Fruitful in this Land

Fruitful in this Land

Pluralism, Dialogue and Healing in
Migrant Pentecostalism

Edited by
André Droogers
Cornelis van der Laan
Wout van Laar

Uitgeverij Boekencentrum, Zoetermeer

www.boekencentrum.nl

Distributed in cooperation with WCC Publications, Geneva

ISBN-13: 978 90 239 1994 0 (Nederland)
ISBN-10: 90 239 1994 7 (Nederland)
ISBN 2-8254-1485-9 (WCC)

NUR 703, 712

Cover design: Oblong, Jet Frenken

© 2006 Uitgeverij Boekencentrum, Zoetermeer, The Netherlands

Table of contents

Introduction: It's Time to get to know Each Other

Wout van Laar

In earlier times, missionaries sailed from Rotterdam harbour bound for a colony or some other distant country. They felt compelled to spread the Gospel overseas. Their journey was from the West to the East and to the South. Those times are past history. Now, evangelists come here from those same countries, to the Netherlands and to other countries in Europe. And with them come thousands more, hoping for freedom, happiness and a future. Rotterdam has large areas where more than half of the population is 'foreign', at least according to official definitions. Non-Western faith communities are flourishing in many parts of the city. In the very places where 30 years ago the Christian presence had almost disappeared, Christianity has staged a comeback. Rotterdam numbers about 95 migrant churches, originating from Africa, Asia and Latin America, many of them with a strong missionary presence. Actually, there are hundreds of migrant churches spread all over the Netherlands.[1]

This reality offers the churches of the West unique opportunities to meet the world church on their own ground. The old European churches are confronted with new faces of Christianity alongside their church buildings and in their parishes. They are being challenged by hitherto unknown expressions of Christian faith, brought from all over the world. Unfamiliar African, Korean, Brazilian and Chinese shapes of Christianity give rainbow-colour to multi-ethnic cities like Rotterdam, Madrid and London.

THE SOUTH COMES NORTH

The multiplicity of migrant churches in Europe reflects the changing conditions on a global scale.

---

1. See Alle Hoekema and Wout van Laar (editors), *The Worldchurch on One Km2. Immigrant Churches in Rotterdam* (Netherlands Missionary Council: Utrecht, 2004), which contains portraits of six migrant churches within one square kilometre in the city's Cool district, the 'secularized' heart of Rotterdam. SKIN, the umbrella organization of more than 50 migrant churches, cites the number of 800,000 migrant Christians living in the Netherlands.

Firstly, enormous shifts in world Christianity during the last decades have been deeply changing the face of the Christian faith. At the beginning of the 21st century, the centre of gravity of the Christian world has definitely shifted from the Northern to the Southern hemisphere. In the South, many churches have been growing explosively. Lamin Sanneh, a theologian from the Gambia, signals two developments that are interconnected: a post-*Christian* West alongside a rapidly increasing post-*Western* Christianity.[2] Churches and their mission offices are not sufficiently aware of the fact that Christianity is once again a non-Western religion. Almost two-thirds of all Christians live in Africa, Asia and Latin America. It is significant that the heart of the Anglican community has shifted to Africa. The Nigerian Church alone has one in four (25%) of all Anglicans worldwide. The overall number of Christians in Africa has increased during the last century from 10 million to 360 million believers. The *World Christian Encyclopedia* states that the present net increase in Africa is 8.4 million Christian believers per year; that is 23,000 believers per day.[3] Black Africa today is totally inconceivable apart from the presence of Christ (Hastings). The reverse is also true: the presence of Christ in our global world is barely conceivable as being separate from its fresh African expressions. The dynamic expressions of faith and witness are those of the people and communities from the less affluent societies on the globe, who respond to the Gospel in their own distinctive ways.

For many centuries, Westerners have tried to impose their own ideas of what Christianity should be, often backed up by the forces of colonial political power and the imposition of patterns and models in line with the fashionable ideologies of Europe. Churches of the South no longer duplicate what has been prompted by the churches of the North. World Christianity today is a variety of indigenous responses to the Gospel that do not *per se* need the European Enlightenment frame. The era of the modern missionary movement is over, and missionary organizations should acknowledge that reality. The traditional Western paradigm of mission presupposed that mission went from the North to the South, from the rich world to the world of the poor, from the centres of power to the margins, from above downwards. This framework also determined the role of the missionary. He or she represented the rich world, carried a bag with money and projects, and was associated with progress, technology and modernity.

Today, we witness the opposite: the mainstream of the missionary movement is going from the South to the North, from the poor world to the rich world, from

---

2. Lamin Sanneh, *Whose Religion is Christianity. The Gospel beyond the West* (Grand Rapids: Eerdmans, 2003).
3. David Barrett et al, *World Christian Encyclopedia: A Comparative Survey of Churches and Religions – AD 30 to 2200* (Oxford: Oxford University Press, 2001).

the margins to the centres of power, from below upwards. What is happening today reminds us of the early Church: the apostle Peter says to the crippled beggar at the temple gate: 'Silver or gold I do not have, but what I have I give you.'[4] It is worth noting that it is not due to some strategy of the apostles that the Gospel reaches the Hellenistic Antioch. Instead, the breakthrough to the non-Jewish world is due to the spontaneous witness of some vulnerable asylum-seekers, who preached in this third city of the Roman Empire that the crucified one is the Lord.[5]

Secondly, the inflow of migrant churches into European countries has to be understood in the context of migration movements from the South to the North. In the present-day world, international migration plays an important albeit often unacknowledged role. In its global dynamics, migration affects every level of public life and is driven by powerful economic, social and political forces. The number of international migrants has increased from 75 million to some 200 million over the past three decades, including 9.2 million refugees. This is equivalent to the present population of the fifth largest country in the world, Brazil. Numbers are increasing rapidly and migrants are now to be found in every part of the world. The number of migrants living in the developed world has reached 110 million (60% of the world's migrants).[6]

It is due to the enormous streams of migration that the Gospel is being carried all over the globe. Much of the time it happens spontaneously, in an unorganised way and beyond the control of the headquarters of mission. More and more Christians from the South are coming to Europe. New Charismatic healing churches are sprouting up in the towns and cities of the West, as far-flung offshoots of the worldwide Christian resurgence. On an average Sunday in cities like London or Amsterdam, one meets more non-Western migrant Christians on their way to places of worship than Christians of 'white' established denominations going to their church buildings. In a matter of a few decades, European Christians have come to be no more than a fragment of non-Western Christianity, where Charismatic and Pentecostal Christians are set to prevail. Christianity in

---

4. Acts 3:6
5. Acts 11:20
6. Statistics from the *Report of Global Commission on International Migration (GCIM)*, 2005, www.gcim.org. In 2000, international migrants were located as follows: 56.1 million in Europe (7.7% of total population), 49.9 million in Asia (1.4%), 40.8 million in North America (12.9%), 16.3 million in Africa (2%), 5.9 million in Latin America (1.1%) and 5.8 million in Australia (18.7%). This means that 1 in 35 people worldwide is an international migrant; or three percent of the world's population. At least 5 million of Europe's 56.1 million migrants in 2000 had irregular status and some 500,000 'undocumented' migrants are estimated to arrive in Europe each year.

this continent is gradually being shaped by the rapidly growing migrant churches or 'diaspora' churches from Africa, Asia and Latin America.

Thirdly, churches and movements of the Charismatic and Pentecostal traditions, in particular, are attracting great numbers and offer new inspiration and hope to millions of people. Pentecostalism could be seen as the fastest growing expression of Christianity of all time. From zero at the start of the 20th century, Pentecostalism tallies over 550 million adherents on the threshold of the 21st century, almost 27 percent of all Christians in 2003. Today, one in four Christians is a Pentecostal believer. As Allan Anderson states, the world's half a billion Pentecostals and charismatics are predominantly Africans, Asians and Latin Americans. The Majority-World continents are where the greatest expansion of Pentecostalism has occurred. We are witnessing a rapid 'pentecostalization' of world Christianity. Europe has to be prepared to respond to this new movement of the Spirit in world history.

How to interpret the phenomenon of the growing non-Western churches in the West? More specifically, how to react to the remarkable growth of Pentecostalism in its vivid manifestations in Europe and the continent's cities? Many established churches still tend to consider migrant churches as exotic leftovers from the ancient 'mission box'. That sometimes results in a condescending attitude: 'conservative' migrant churches should first be upgraded theologically before they are acceptable in the 'progressive' ecumenical movement. Others condemn non-Western Pentecostalism as if it were some questionable by-product of Western imperialism in the 'Third World'. In Latin America, Pentecostalism was for a long time stigmatised as 'dollar–Protestantism', exported from and promoted by the United States for political reasons. It could be more realistic to welcome the variety and vitality of those 'Spirit' churches as outposts of future Christianity and as a remarkable gift of God to a secularised world, which desperately longs for a new sense of life and hope.

ENCOUNTER IN MISSIOLOGICAL PERSPECTIVE

Turning to the Netherlands, an interesting story can be told. In 1996, the delegates of the Netherlands Missionary Council (*Nederlandse Zendingsraad*, NZR)[7]

---

7. The NZR is a platform of about 20 Dutch denominations and organizations for the exchange of reflections and ideas on mission in its broadest meaning. Most of the affiliated organizations are from an ecumenical or evangelical background. The umbrella organization of migrant churches, SKIN, also participates. For a complete list of the participants and more information, consult the council's Dutch website at *www.zendingsraad.nl*.

were amazed that there were no representatives of the Afro-Brazilian Pentecostal churches at the Conference on World Mission and Evangelism in Salvador, Brazil. When they questioned the conference leadership about this, they were challenged by the latter and by the staff of the World Council of Churches in Geneva, to start a dialogue with the national Pentecostal and Charismatic organizations back home.

Together with the Evangelical Missionary Alliance (*Evangelische Zendingsalliantie*, EZA) and the Roman Catholic Mission Council (*Nederlandse Missieraad*, NMR), the NZR organised a 'day of meeting and consultation' in May 1998. This consultation brought together Christian leaders of the Ecumenical, Evangelical, Charismatic and Pentecostal traditions, 'in the hope that in this meeting and celebration a new vision may grow for cooperation and unity in the one mission of God (*Missio Dei*)'.[8] More than 50 representatives of these various traditions took part, including members of the migrant churches. This initiative resulted, in January 1999, in the formation of the Missionary Quarterly Council (*Missionair Kwartaalberaad*). The participants agreed to 'initiate a learning process in which we get to know one another in such a way that it will remove our prejudices and lead to possible ways of cooperation in a missiological perspective'. Ultimate goal is to develop a framework for a common missionary strategy for the 21st century.[9]

During the process of dialogue which followed, a wide range of topics was discussed.[10] One of the most significant features of this dialogue was the time of worship and prayer, usually at the beginning of each session. Looking back on the process, the chairman concluded: 'What cannot be reported are the experiences during the moments of celebration and fellowship, which are the heart of the Missionary Quarterly Council; those recurring moments, when we light the candle and are silent together in the face of God and call out his name. When we worship him, it brings the participants closer to one another and these moments are invaluable.'[11]

The quarterly meetings culminated in an international symposium on 'Non-Western Pentecostalism in the Netherlands', held February 27-29, 2003, in Amsterdam. The first day of this symposium was held at a location in the city's Bijlmer

---

8. Wout van Laar, *Missionair Kwartaalberaad – Een Terugblik*, NZR document 123/01 (Amsterdam: Nederlandse Zendingsraad, 2001) p. 1.
9. Wout van Laar, *Missionair Kwartaalberaad – Een Terugblik*, p. 2.
10. For more details, see the article of Paul van der Laan, *Guidelines for a challenging dialogue*, in this book.
11. Wout van Laar, *Missionair Kwartaalberaad – Een Terugblik*, p. 9.

suburb, home to many of the migrant churches. On the second day, the participants came together at the *Vrije Universiteit Amsterdam* for reflection on the three
case studies of Pentecostal churches in the Bijlmer, which are predominantly
African, Asian and Latin American in ethnic composition. This symposium took
place in conjunction with the institution of the Pentecostal Academic Chair (Cornelis van der Laan was inaugurated as Professor of Pentecostalism) and the formal opening of the Hollenweger Center for the Interdisciplinary Study of
Pentecostal and Charismatic Movements, both at the *Vrije Universiteit Amsterdam*.[12]

The contributions to this publication originated from the meetings of the Missionary Quarterly Council held between 1999 and the Amsterdam symposium in
2003. Questions that were being dealt with include: in what way does the proliferation and variety of Pentecostalism challenge Western Christianity? What does
the presence of non-Western Pentecostalism have to say to the 'mainline' churches
in the West? What about the dialogue between 'Ecumenicals' and Pentecostals
at the global level, at the continental (European) level and particularly in the
Netherlands, with its strong Reformed tradition. How does the Christianity of
the Enlightenment relate to expressions of Christian faith that are less determined
by *ratio* and modernity, or which even involve thinking and acting within a pre-
modern framework? How do these non-Western churches and communities live
and witness in secularised and post-modern societies? How do they themselves
see their role (and the role of religion and faith) in societies where growing xenophobia seems to be more powerful than tolerance and hospitality? Could 'old'
and 'new' churches together – amid brokenness and in conflict situations – find
common, contemporary forms of healing ministry, inspired by the 'healing communities' that many of the churches of the South represent for their members
and for others?

PLURALISM

This book is structured around three major themes: pluralism, dialogue and healing. A diversity of authors, each of them in some way involved in the dialogue
with migrant churches and with Pentecostalism, delve into the subject, throwing
light from various angles on issues related to migrant Pentecostalism. They try
to find some direction in this, for the most part, unworked field of investigation.

When reading the various contributions to this publication, it becomes evident
that Pentecostalism represents a multifarious phenomenon. Drawing on his

---

12. The Hollenweger Center is a cooperative entity of the VU faculties of Theology and
    of Social Sciences, and the Azusa Theological Seminary.

global survey of Pentecostalism in Africa, Asia and Latin America, Allan Anderson points out its endless pluralism. Nevertheless, in all its variety, the Pentecostal faith has meaning for people in the most diverse, concrete life situations. It demonstrates 'enacted theology' or 'theology in practice'. It is to be found in the preaching, rituals and practices of churches that have contextualised Christianity all over the world in such a way as to make it really meaningful to ordinary people.

Cornelis van der Laan presents a panorama of the migrant churches in the Netherlands, in particular the non-Western Pentecostal churches. He gives attention to their relationship with the Dutch churches and society, and to some of the missiological questions they raise. Van der Laan concludes that, while many become disappointed in their expectation of finding our part of the world to be a land of milk and honey, they keep on 'knocking on heaven's door'. And many of them find a home in the migrant churches, which for them are places of belonging, islands of hope in the midst of a harsh, secularised Western world.

In his introduction to the various strands of Dutch Pentecostalism, Huibert Zegwaart affirms that the diversity of the movement in this country may to a considerable degree be attributed to its international orientation. It is this particular trait that gives cause for hope about the possible integration of the migrant churches with the indigenous movement in the near future. Only time will tell as to which of the two following tendencies will become dominant within Dutch Pentecostalism: one in which 'Pentecost behind the dikes' will remain divided by newly-dug canals; or the other, whereby efforts to unify result in bridges being built across the demarcation lines.

Claudia Währisch-Oblau gives a typology of non-Western churches in Europe based on the German context. She proposes to stop using terms like 'foreigners' churches' or 'migrant churches', and replace them with 'new mission churches'. The Nigerian pastor Rufus Ositulu (Aladura Church) describes the mission of migrant churches in Europe as follows: 'They have a task here, which is to win new and lost souls for Jesus Christ ..., for those to whom Christ was once preached have now come back to the areas from which the original preachers set off, to preach Christ in all his goodness to all inhabitants of these areas.' Their members do not see themselves as exiles bent on returning to their home country, but rather identify with the former slaves in Egypt who were brought by God into the Promised Land. They have a right to be here, even if officials or governments tell them that this is not the case. Their vision is clear: 'We shall be fruitful in this land' (Gen 26.22).

DIALOGUE

The second section deals with the dialogue between the 'mainline' ecumenical churches and the Pentecostal movement. Huibert van Beek describes how two worldwide movements, which during the last century have taken separate courses – away from each other and ignoring each other – arrived at a new point of departure as the century moved into its final decade: the ecumenical movement of the World Council of Churches and the Pentecostal movement found each other in the start of a promising dialogue. This process resulted in the 'Joint Consultative Group of the WCC and Pentecostals', which began its work in 1999 and meets annually.

Cheryl Bridges Johns poses a challenging question: what can the 'mainline' learn from the Pentecostals about Pentecost? She points out that Pentecost belongs to the whole church and not to any particular group. Pentecostalism reminds the world church of the dramatic implications of Pentecost. To celebrate Pentecost is not to recall an event that is locked in time and space. Rather, it is to participate in a continuing festival that is ever more mysterious, frightening and wonderful than we can ever dare to imagine. The modern church seems obsessed with a desire to be central, to have voice and influence. Pentecost mocks all attempts to contain power, calls us to relinquish this desire for centrality, and marginalises all who dare to participate. The liberating power of the Spirit is most clearly experienced in the margins.

Paul van der Laan summarises what lessons can be learned from recent dialogues in the Netherlands in which he personally participated. He praises the ecumenical dialogue that flourished in his home country after 1988, as having surpassed his wildest dreams. Van der Laan first goes into the details of the dialogue with the Reformed Churches in the Netherlands. He then focuses on the initial history of the dialogue in missiological perspective, started by the Netherlands Missionary Council in 1999, and refers to the conferences of the Roman Catholic Charismatics. Van der Laan concludes by drawing on his experiences to offer some practical guidelines for a challenging dialogue with Pentecostals.

A more theological reflection is to be found in the article by Cornelis van der Kooi. He affirms that the rise and spread of Pentecostal and Charismatic Christianity worldwide puts the traditional churches in a position that in many respects requires a theological re-orientation. The latter are confronted with a vital Pentecostal Christianity that is of non-Western origin and whose forms of Christian faith are unfamiliar to the traditional churches. The challenge lies in the fact that Western Christians have to deal with a Christianity that does not bear the hallmarks of modernity. The 'mainline' churches should be prepared to recognise the migrant churches in their sometimes pre-modern worldview, as partners of the one body of Christ, which should not be upgraded theologically as a pre-condition for engaging in dialogue.

HEALING

The third section brings together reflections on churches as healing communities. Healing is an integral part of church life in the South and not only in Pentecostal churches. Wout van Laar turns to the churches of the Southern hemisphere to find out about the distinctive ways in which those churches go about healing. It is worth the effort to gather in-depth knowledge of the insights and intuitions from Africa, Asia and Latin America. Healing as practiced by Jesus is closer to the everyday life of non-Western Christians than for children of the Enlightenment. The many migrant churches in Amsterdam offer 'healing places', meeting-points of hope and love for the marginalised in desolate suburbs like the Bijlmer.

Richard Shaull responded to a previous text of this article during what was to become his last visit to Europe, some months before his death in 2002. Shaull gave some experienced reflections on the wounded healer from the perspective of his personal involvement in Brazil in recent years. Over a long period of time, we in the West have seen ourselves as those who are the bearers of a healing ministry to the peoples of other lands. The stark reality is that this dynamic message of bringing healing to broken people and to a broken world, is evident primarily among the poor in the South – not in the West. The 'mainline' churches have to re-situate themselves among the poor, in their neighbourhood and elsewhere, and be prepared to enter into their religious realm. They should be open to the witness of the poor to the rich world. Therefore, a new theological paradigm is required.

A vivid illustration of healing ministry is the personal witness of Daniel Himmans-Arday about God's healing power in the True Teachings of Christ's Temple, one of the flourishing Ghanaian churches in the Bijlmer. Two 'intermezzos' – miniature portraits of Pentecostal spirituality – complete this book: Cornelis van der Laan introduces the reader to The House of Fellowship, an African Pentecostal church also in the Bijlmer; and, in a short but meaningful article, Walter Hollenweger offers some humorous images from the 'missiologists' Matthew and Luke.

In his 'prospective epilogue', André Droogers considers the book's three sub-themes – pluralism, dialogue and healing – in their interconnectedness, as a cultural anthropologist of religion. The author underlines that the Power of the Spirit cannot be understood without discussing the Spirit of Power. He reconsiders power and meaning in their relevance to the understanding of Pentecostalism and especially in its migrant version. The migrant churches are perhaps privileged in being marginal according to almost all definitions. They may show an alternative model of power which paradoxically demonstrates that it is difficult to domesticate the power of the Spirit, despite the spirit of power.

As editors, we are grateful to be able to publish this book as a common publication of the Hollenweger Center for the Interdisciplinary Study of Pentecostal and Charismatic Movements at the *Vrije Universiteit Amsterdam* and the Netherlands Missionary Council (NZR) in Utrecht. This reflects the spirit of cooperation between the different institutions in the Netherlands with regard to the significance of global Pentecostalism for the mainline churches and the *oikoumene*.

Pentecostal spirituality shows a contagious passion for the Kingdom. The witness of Pentecostals might inspire the mainline churches to move beyond where they are, in their experience of a God who compassionately loves his world. It's time to get to know each other. That involves listening carefully to the challenging voice of one of the present generation's Pentecostal theologians:

Perhaps God has raised up the rough-hewn, largely immature but passionate Pentecostals in this century to remind the church of the apocalyptic power and force of the gospel of the kingdom and to prepare the world for the end – the triune God who is to be "all in all". This church which is filled with the Spirit and immersed in the compassionate care of the lost and afflicted humanity has one common longing, one unifying cry, one joyful shout: Come, Lord Jesus![13]

A special word of thank goes to Andreas Havinga. As an experienced English-language consultant, he proofread and prepared the articles in this book with great accuracy and dedication.

---

13. Steven J. Land, *Pentecostal Spirituality. A Passion for the Kingdom*, Sheffield: Sheffield Academic Press 1993, p. 219.

I PLURALISM

1. The Proliferation and Varieties of Pentecostalism in the Majority World

Allan Anderson

DEFINING 'PENTECOSTALISM'

Pentecostalism, with origins in the late 19th and early 20th centuries, has become probably the fastest growing expression of Christianity of all time. Statisticians David Barrett and Todd Johnson estimated that there were over 553 million 'Pentecostals / charismatics / neocharismatics' – almost 27 percent of the Christians in the world in 2003 – and projected this to rise to 31 percent by 2025.[1] These impressive but speculative figures are often quoted to point to 'Pentecostalism', the largest force in world Christianity after Roman Catholicism.[2] But the half a billion 'Pentecostals / charismatics / neocharismatics' are predominantly Asians, Africans and Latin Americans – and female. The Majority-World continents are where the greatest expansion of Pentecostalism has occurred.

Pentecostalism is best understood as multifarious movements concerned primarily with the experience of the working of the Spirit and the practice of spiritual gifts. In this sense, the term would include at least three categories: (1) 'classical' or 'denominational' Pentecostals originating in the North American Holiness Movement, with historical links to the Azusa Street Revival in Los Angeles (1906-1908); (2) the Charismatic movement in the older churches, still a force to be reckoned with; and (3) the independent and indigenous churches, 'fellowships' and 'ministries' whose members now form the majority of Pentecostals worldwide. The 'classical' Pentecostals (like the Assemblies of God and the Church of God) are also a very active and growing phenomenon throughout the world and have played a significant role in the emergence of some of the more recent groups. The Charismatic movement is still an enormous phenomenon in the Majority World, especially in the Roman Catholic Church.

---

1. David B. Barrett and Todd M. Johnson, 'Annual Statistical Table on Global Mission: 2003'. In: *International Bulletin of Missionary Research* 27/1 (January 2003) p. 25.
2. Gary B. McGee, 'Pentecostal Missiology: Moving beyond Triumphalism to Face the Issues'. In: *Pneuma* 16/2 (1994) p. 276.

Statistics on a macro level are notoriously speculative and difficult to verify. Although scholars have great difficulties with Barrett and Johnson's statistics, at face value they illustrate that Pentecostal and Charismatic movements have many different forms all over the world. Yet at the same time, it is important to understand the authors' inclusive and globalized definition of 'Pentecostal / Charismatic / Neocharismatic'. How this is defined is crucial to analysing these statistics.

It is clear that Barrett and Johnson do not assume that the term is referring mainly to the denominational Pentecostals with roots in North America. By far the largest group included in their term is what they call a 'megabloc' of 394 million 'Independents', which have the 'synonymous alternate terms' of 'Postdenominationalists' and 'neo-Apostolics'. The statisticians explained in 2001 that this new 'megabloc' included the 'non-white indigenous' category in their earlier tables.[3] Of course, there are obvious difficulties with this broad classification, and understanding the terms 'Pentecostal / Charismatic' is greatly affected by it. Among many other groups included are the majority of African Initiated Churches (AICs), and a large number of Chinese independent churches.[4]

Pentecostalism's strengths lie especially in an ability to adjust and 'incarnate' in any culture, and so the particular, local expressions of Pentecostalism (the 'Pentecostalisms') are more important than any 'global' or 'supra-cultural' quality of 'Pentecostalism'. Its emphasis on the 'freedom of the Spirit' militates against any homogenizing or dispassionate standardizing tendencies that one sometimes finds in the writings of the globalization theorists.

Nevertheless, access to modern electronic media, communications and rapid travel, and the consequential interdependence of Pentecostals and Charismatics the world over, have resulted in certain commonalities within the Pentecostal and Charismatic movements themselves that have affected their local character. This is particularly true of the emphasis on the power and gifts of the Spirit, and the sense and experience of the immediacy of God that pervades Pentecostalism throughout the globe. But it is also found in such characteristics as an emphasis on prayer, a high view of the Bible, participation of all believers in Christian service and witness, the use of an indigenous leadership, and a conservative Christian morality.

---

3. David B Barrett & Todd M Johnson 2001. 'Annual Statistical Table on Global Mission: 2001'. In: *International Bulletin of Missionary Research* 25/1 (January 2001) p. 24.
4. Allan Anderson, *Moya: The Holy Spirit in an African Context,* Pretoria, University of South Africa Press, 1991; Allan Anderson & Samuel Otwang, *Tumelo: The Faith of African Pentecostals in South Africa* (Pretoria: University of South Africa Press, 1993).

But this is not a one-way street, an unstoppable process of homogenisation. The so-called 'global culture' is itself changed and formed by its encounter with local contexts. 'Globalization' must not be construed to mean an overarching domination of an 'international culture' that neatly separates the 'global' from the 'local' and, in this context, is often seen as the 'Americanization' of Christianity. In fact, 'globalization' is both defined and limited by the local context. All the common features of Pentecostalism, like those mentioned above, are reinterpreted and conditioned by the social and religio-cultural context, and this is also true of migrant churches in the West.

Many movements throughout the world (like AICs) are 'Pentecostal' movements that have developed forms of Christianity quite different from Western Pentecostalism. This indigenous Christianity has been assimilated into local cultures more easily than older forms of European and North American Christianity were. This does not mean that these forms of Christianity are more 'authentic' than other Christian churches are. But it does demonstrate Pentecostal spirituality interacting with popular beliefs and practices. We will look at this phenomenon in three different continents.

PENTECOSTALISM IN LATIN AMERICA

The rapid growth of Pentecostalism in Latin America in the second half of the 20th century has been one of the most remarkable stories in the history of Christianity. It has been most extensively studied, particularly by sociologists. A conservatively estimated 10 percent of Latin America's population are now Pentecostal/ Charismatic/ neo-Charismatic. In Colombia, Puerto Rico, El Salvador, Argentina and Guatemala the figure might be over 20 percent, and in Chile and Brazil over 30 percent.[5]

The first Pentecostals in South America were Argentines and Chileans. The origin of Chilean Pentecostalism is associated with Willis C. Hoover (1856-1936), a North American revivalist minister in Valparaiso, pastor of the largest Methodist congregation in Chile and a district superintendent. Significantly, the Chilean movement was not connected to North American Pentecostalism, and Hoover became founder of an autonomous and indigenous Chilean church in 1909. To the present day, his Methodist Pentecostal Church (MPC), the largest Pentecostal church in Chile, has maintained its Methodist doctrines and practices, including infant baptism and other Methodist structures.

---

5. E.A. Wilson, 'Latin America', S.M. Burgess and E.M. van der Maas (eds). In: *New International Dictionary of Pentecostal and Charismatic Movements* (Grand Rapids, MI: Zondervan, 2002) p. 158.

This closeness to Methodism differentiates Chilean Pentecostalism from classical Pentecostalism from North America.[6] In addition, Chilean Pentecostalism did not follow classical Pentecostalism's doctrine of 'initial evidence'. Edward Cleary thinks that Chilean Pentecostalism represents 'the first self-sufficient church in the Third World'. Chilean Pentecostalism, unlike some other forms of Protestantism, has succeeded in attracting the lower classes and indigenous Americans into its ranks, but is increasingly becoming middle class. Chilean Pentecostal churches were also the first Pentecostal groups ever to join the World Council of Churches.[7]

Juan Sepúlveda says that Chilean Pentecostalism – one of the earliest expressions of the movement in the world to arise independently of North American Pentecostalism – is an expression of indigenous Christianity in Latin America. In particular, Chilean Pentecostalism was able to translate its message into the forms of popular Chilean culture and to spread among the poor masses. Sepúlveda's view reinforces the contention that Pentecostalism's ability to adapt to any cultural context is one of its main strengths.[8]

Argentine Pentecostalism made rapid progress in the 1990s, and by 2000 had 18 million adherents or 23 percent of the population, compared with Chile's 5,5 million or 36 percent of the population, according to one source.[9]

Brazil today has one of the highest numbers of Pentecostals in the world.[10] There are probably more Pentecostals in church on Sundays in Brazil than Catholics, and more Pentecostal pastors (all Brazilian) than Catholic priests, who are often foreigners.[11] The *Assembléias de Deus* (Assemblies of God) in Brazil is today the largest Protestant church in Latin America, with some 14 million members in 2000, among 79 million Brazilian 'Pentecostals / Charismatics / independents' that form 40 percent of the total population, according to one estimate.[12]

---

6. Juan Sepúlveda, 'Indigenous Pentecostalism and the Chilean Experience'. In: Allan H Anderson and Walter J Hollenweger (eds), *Pentecostals After a Century: Global Perspectives on a Movement in Transition* (Sheffield, UK: Sheffield Academic Press, 1999) p. 117.
7. E.L. Cleary and H.W. Stewart-Gambino (eds). *Power, Politics and Pentecostals in Latin America*. (Boulder, CO: Westview Press, 1997) pp. 97, 111, 113.
8. Sepúlveda, 'Indigenous Pentecostalism', pp. 112-5, 118, 120, 124, 126-133.
9. Wilson, 'Latin America', p. 158; Cleary, pp. 106, 110.
10. Phillip Berryman, *Religion in the Megacity: Catholic and Protestant portraits from Latin America* (New York: Orbis, 1996) p. 42.
11. Harvey Cox, *Fire from Heaven: The Rise of Pentecostal Spirituality and the Reshaping of religion in the Twenty-first Century* (London: Cassell, 1996) pp. 168, 175.
12. E.A. Wilson, 'Brazil'. In: Burgess and van der Maas, *New International Dictionary*, pp. 35, 38.

The Assemblies of God considers itself an independent church within the world-wide Assemblies of God fellowship of churches. Members were recruited initially from the lower strata of society, and Pentecostals appealed to black, mixed race and Amerindian Brazilians. Mulattos are still the majority in this denomination – there are more black Brazilians in Pentecostal churches than in any other denomination.[13] The Assemblies of God has education and literacy programmes for members; provident funds for unmarried mothers, the sick and the orphaned; printed literature from their own publishing house; and projects like community centres, factories, schools, hospitals, old age homes, libraries and day nurseries.[14]

It is estimated that a second phase of 20-30 new Brazilian Pentecostal denominations arose during the 1950s (the 'modern' phase), the most important being *Brasil para Cristo* (Brazil for Christ, BPC), the *Igreja Pentecostal Deus É Amor* (God is Love Pentecostal Church, DEA) and the *Igreja do Evangelho Quadrangular* (Foursquare Gospel Church, IEQ).[15] BPC developed good relations with other churches and is a member of the World Council of Churches.[16]

After about 1975, a third type of Pentecostal movement began in what Chesnut calls the 'postmodern' era, the largest being the *Igreja Universal do Reino de Deus* (Universal Church of the Kingdom of God, IURD). This is a prosperity-oriented healing movement, founded in 1977 in Rio de Janeiro by Bishop Edir Macedo, a former state lottery official. By the early 1990s, the IURD, which concentrates on the middle class, was the fastest growing church in Brazil, with 1,000 churches, over a million adherents by some estimates, and a TV station costing 45 million US dollars. The church emphasises healing, prosperity, collective exorcisms from Umbanda spirits and other demons, and a 'dramatic display of spiritual power'. This church, with perhaps four million affiliates in 2000, has expanded its operations into other countries worldwide.[17]

The most dramatic Pentecostal growth of all has taken place in Central America, and especially in Guatemala, with the island of Puerto Rico now perhaps the most Protestant nation in Latin America. Guatemala has over two million Pentecostals, almost half of who are indigenous Maya.[18] The largest non-Catholic denomination in Central America is the Assemblies of God, with closer links to

13. Berryman, p. 17; David Martin, *Tongues of Fire: The Explosion of Protestantism in Latin America* (Oxford: Basil Blackwell, 1990) p. 67.
14. Hollenweger, *The Pentecostals* (London: SCM, 1973) p. 80.
15. R. Andrew Chesnut, *Born Again in Brazil: The Pentecostal Boom and the Pathogens of Poverty* (New Brunswick: Rutgers University Press) p. 35; Berryman, p. 30.
16. Wilson, 'Latin America', p. 159; Martin, p. 66; Chesnut, pp. 36-38; Berryman, p. 31.
17. Wilson, 'Latin America', p. 159; Berryman, pp. 33-34; Chesnut, pp. 45-47.
18. Johnstone and Mandryk, p. 288.

the USA than the Brazilian one; but Petersen points out that this is not a dependent relationship, for there is only one foreign missionary for every 25,000 members.[19]

Remarkable Pentecostal growth is also taking place in the Caribbean. In Puerto Rico (26 precent), Jamaica (19 percent), Trinidad (11 percent) and Haiti (7 percent), the Pentecostal movement represents a significant proportion of the population, with denominations often having North American connections. Pentecostalism was planted in Puerto Rico by Juan L. Lugo (1890-1984), a Puerto Rican converted in Hawaii in 1907 by missionaries from Azusa Street. In 1921, he founded what is now the largest non-Catholic denomination in the island, the Pentecostal Church of God of Puerto Rico (PCG).

The PCG sends missionaries all over Latin America as well as to Spain and Portugal.[20] The Church of God (Cleveland) sent its first missionaries to the Bahamas in 1907 and to Jamaica in 1918, where it is now the largest Pentecostal denomination, known as the New Testament Church of God, followed by the Church of God of Prophecy.[21] These two denominations were taken to England by Jamaican immigrants in the 1950s, and are the largest black-led denominations in the UK.

Latin American and Caribbean Pentecostalism (as elsewhere) is extremely diverse with many schisms, and any assessment must beware of generalisations. Statistics vary enormously, but an estimated half of the classical Pentecostals in the world are Latin Americans. There were an estimated 141 million Latin American Pentecostals/ Charismatics/ neo-Pentecostals in 2000, of which half were in Brazil alone.[22] According to present growth rates, several Latin American countries could have a majority of non-Catholics (mostly Pentecostals) by 2010.[23] Pope John Paul II warned against the 'invasion of the sects' and the 'ravenous wolves' that were threatening the traditional Catholic hold on Latin America.[24]

And yet, Pentecostalism in Latin America is fundamentally an indigenous phenomenon. Recent studies show that Catholicism has proportionately far more foreign priests in Latin America (an astonishing 94 percent in Venezuela) than

19. Douglas Petersen, *Not by Might nor by Power: A Pentecostal Theology of Social Concern in Latin America* (Oxford: Regnum, 1996) p. 62.
20. D.D. Bundy, 'Puerto Rico', Burgess and van der Maas, pp. 209-210; Cleary, pp. 164-166.
21. D.D. Bundy, 'Jamaica (II)', Burgess and van der Maas, pp. 146-7.
22. Wilson, 'Latin America', pp. 157-158.
23. Cox, p. 168.
24. Cleary, p. 228.

Pentecostal churches have foreign missionaries.[25] Many Pentecostal denominations were founded in Latin America before the major ones in the USA, from which they are sometimes erroneously presumed to have emerged. As Harvey Cox observes, in all the different interpretations of the causes for the growth of Pentecostals, few will admit 'with Saint Peter' that it is 'evidence of the activity of the Spirit',[26] an observation that might be applied to Pentecostalism's growth in other parts of the Majority World!

PENTECOSTALS IN AFRICA

Several thousand African initiated church (AIC) organizations throughout the sub-Sahara region go by various names, and do not usually call themselves 'Pentecostal' or 'Charismatic'. In southern Africa, the majority of them are known as 'Zionist' and 'Apostolic' churches; throughout Africa they are 'churches of the Spirit'; and in western Nigeria *'Aladura'* ('prayer') churches. In addition to these churches, there are a great number of rapidly growing newer independent Pentecostal or Charismatic churches and 'ministries' throughout the continent, which are also 'African initiated' churches. These are often the most prominent type of Pentecostalism brought from Africa to the Western world. In several African countries, these are becoming the dominant form of Christianity, and in some nations, AICs of different types together form the majority of Christians – an extremely important component of world Christianity.

The 'churches of the Spirit' have much in common with other Pentecostals. They all practise gifts of the Spirit like healing, prophecy and speaking in tongues. But because of their 'Spirit' manifestations, their pneumatic emphases and experiences, most early studies of these churches in the African context considered them 'syncretistic', 'post-Christian' and 'messianic'. Part of the problem that Western observers had with the 'churches of the Spirit' had to do with their pneumatology. It is important to understand this, as this was often seen as accommodating the pre-Christian past, and in particular was thought to be linked with traditional divination, ancestor rituals and the like. Some observers spoke of them as having 'misunderstood' the Holy Spirit.[27] But it is now increasingly recognised that far from being a 'misunderstanding', these and many other indigenous

---

25. Cleary, p. 231.
26. Cox, pp. 163-7, 171-4, 177-8.
27. Allan Anderson, *Zion and Pentecost: The Spirituality and Experience of Pentecostal and Zionist/ Apostolic Churches in South Africa* (Pretoria: University of South Africa Press, 2000) pp. 241-2; Marthinus L. Daneel, *Fambidzano: Ecumenical Movement of Zimbabwean Independent Churches* (Gweru, Zimbabwe: Mambo Press, 1989) pp. 329-330, 340.

churches have made an important contribution to the inculturation of Pentecostal theology.

An estimated 11 percent of Africa's total population (including the predominantly Muslim north) was 'Charismatic' in 2000.[28] Classical Pentecostals have
been operating in Africa since 1907, and the Assemblies of God in particular has
grown in almost every African country, with over four million members estimated
in 1994.[29] Pentecostal churches are actively growing throughout Africa, particularly in Zimbabwe, where they were 20 percent of the population in 2000, Kenya
(14 percent), Nigeria (11 percent), Ghana (10 percent), Zambia (10 percent), the
DR Congo (8 percent) and South Africa (8 percent). If the other forms of African
Pentecostalism as defined here are taken into account, then the figures would be
considerably higher: Zimbabwe 56 percent, South Africa 46 percent, Kenya 36
percent, Congo 30 percent, Nigeria 29 percent, Ghana 29 percent and Zambia
25 percent.[30] These figures, though necessarily speculative, indicate the strength
of African Pentecostalism today.

Most AICs are of a Pentecostal type that have contextualized Christianity in
Africa.[31] Although these older African churches might no longer be paradigmatic
of African Pentecostalism, they are certainly an important expression of it. There
are several thousands of these churches throughout the sub-Sahara region that
go by many different names. In several African countries, African independent
churches form the majority of Christians.[32]

The AIC Pentecostals differ from other Pentecostals in several ways. There are
external differences like the use of healing symbols including blessed water, other
symbolic ritual objects representing power and protection, forms of government
and patterns of leadership, the use of some African cultural practices and the
wearing of distinctive church apparel. But they also differ fundamentally in their
approach to African religions and culture, in liturgy, in healing practices and in
their unique contribution to Christianity in a broader African context. This distinct and innovative approach often differs sharply from those Pentecostals who
are more heavily influenced by Western Pentecostalism. Although there are clear

28. P. Johnstone and J Mandryck, *Operation World*, (Carlisle, UK: Paternoster, 2001) p.
    21.
29. Everett A. Wilson, *Strategy of the Spirit: J Philip Hogan and the Growth of the Assem-
    blies of God Worldwide 1960-1990* (Carlisle, UK: Regnum, 1997) p. 119.
30. Johnstone and Mandryk.
31. Cox, p. 246.
32. Anderson, *Zion and Pentecost*; Allan Anderson, *African Reformation: African Initi-
    ated Christianity in the Twentieth Century* (Trenton, NJ and Asmara, Eritrea: Africa
    World Press, 2001).

affinities and common historical and theological origins shared by African and Western Pentecostals, the passing of time and the proliferation of AICs may have accentuated the differences.[33] Pentecostal AICs are found throughout Africa, and are often churches that emphasise healing through prophets.[34]

New Pentecostal and Charismatic churches (NPCs), which have only sprung up since the 1970s, are fast becoming a major expression of Christianity on the continent, especially in the cities, and are often the most prominent form of African Pentecostalism transplanted in Europe and North America by African immigrants. NPCs began to emerge all over Africa in the 1980s, particularly in West Africa, where they tend to have a more educated leadership and membership, including professionals. Their services are usually emotional, enthusiastic and loud, especially as most NPCs make use of electronic musical instruments. Some NPCs propagate a 'prosperity gospel', but identifying NPCs with North American Pentecostalism fails to appreciate the reconstructions and innovations made by these movements in adapting to radically different contexts.[35]

Methods employed by NPCs, like those of other Pentecostals, include door-to-door evangelism, 'cottage meetings' held in homes of inquirers, preaching in trains, buses, on street corners and at places of public concourse, and in 'tent crusades', both large and small, held all over the continent. Many NPCs arose in the context of interdenominational and evangelical campus and school Christian organisations, such as Scripture Union. The emergence of these NPCs indicates that there are unresolved questions facing the Church in Africa, such as the role of 'success' and 'prosperity' in God's economy, enjoying God and his gifts, including healing and material provision, and the holistic dimension of 'salvation' that is meaningful in an African context.[36]

'Pentecostalism' In Asia

Indications are that the fastest growing form of Christianity throughout Asia is of a Pentecostal type and that 'Charismatic' Christianity dominates the older

---

33. Anderson, *Zion and Pentecost,* pp. 27-28.
34. Further details on all these movements can be found in Anderson, *African Reformation,* pp. 69-190.
35. Paul Gifford (ed.), *New Dimensions in African Christianity* (Nairobi: All Africa Conference of Churches, 1992) pp. 8, 24.
36. Anderson, *African Reformation,* pp. 82-186; Allan Anderson, 'The New Pentecostal and Charismatic Churches: The Shape of Future Christianity in Africa?' In: *Pneuma, The Journal of the Society for Pentecostal Studies* 24/2 (Fall 2002) pp. 167-184.

churches, both Protestant and Catholic.[37] Barrett and Johnson estimate that Asia is second only to Latin America in the continents of the world as far as numbers of 'renewal members' is concerned, with almost 135 million in 2000.[38] Harvey Cox speaks of 'the rapid spread of the Spirit-oriented forms of Christianity in Asia';[39] and one can now speak of the 'Pentecostalisation' of Asian Christianity, particularly among Chinese, Korean, Filipino and Indian churches. It was estimated that Christians formed almost nine percent of the population of Asia in 2000, amounting to some 382 million people. Of this number, some 87 million 'Charismatics' constituted 23 percent of the Christian population.[40] The extent of Pentecostal forms of Christianity in the religious diversity of Asia has seldom been recognised.

There were an estimated 33 million Charismatics and Pentecostals in India in 2000, exceeded only by Brazil, the USA, China and Nigeria.[41] The majority of these are in South India. Pentecostalism is clearly the fastest growing form of Christianity in what will soon be the most populous nation on earth. Indonesia has had an amazing story of Christian growth in a majority Muslim country. Many of the largest churches there are home-grown Indonesian churches that have emerged as flourishing churches without links to the Western world.[42] There are at least nine million Pentecostals and Charismatics in Indonesia, amounting to four percent of the total population in a country that is 80 percent Muslim.[43] In 2000, three of the largest non-Catholic churches in Indonesia were Pentecostal, one of which, the Pentecostal Church of Indonesia, had 1.4 million adherents.[44]

Several Filipino missionaries who converted to Pentecostalism in the USA, were the founders of Pentecostalism in the Philippines. Pentecostals there have grown to such an extent that they are regarded as a serious challenge to the Catholic Church.[45] The three largest Pentecostal churches are the Jesus is Lord Fellow-

---

37. Hwa Yung, 'Pentecostalism and the Asian Church'. In: Allan Anderson & Edmond Tang (eds.), *Asian and Pentecostal: The Charismatic Face of Christianity in Asia*, 2003, forthcoming, ch. 3.
38. D.B. Barrett and T.M. Johnson, 'Global Statistics'. In: Burgess & van der Maas (eds.), *New International Dictionary*, p. 287.
39. Cox, p. 214.
40. Johnstone and Mandryk, p. 41.
41. Stanley M. Burgess, 'Pentecostalism in India: An Overview'. In: *Asian Journal of Pentecostal Studies* 4/1 (2001) p. 85.
42. Gani Wiyono, 'Pentecostalism in Indonesia'; and Mark Robinson, 'The Growth of Indian Pentecostalism'. In: Anderson & Tang, *Asian and Pentecostal,* chs. 13 and 14.
43. Burgess and van der Maas, p. 126.
44. Johnstone and Mandryk, p. 339.
45. Robert C. Salazar (ed), *New Religious Movements in Asia and the Pacific Islands: implications for church and society* (Manila: De La Salle University, 1994) p. 190.

ship founded by Ed Villaneuva in 1978, the Jesus Miracle Crusade (both these are Filipino-founded churches) and the Assemblies of God; but there are many other churches, totalling some two million members and perhaps four million affiliates in 2000.[46] But dwarfing all these churches is the Catholic Charismatic movement of Mike Velarde, *El Shaddai*, with some eight million members. There are also more distinctly indigenous Filipino movements of a Pentecostal character, such as the *Santuala* movement among the mountain peoples of Luzon that has combined Filipino pre-Christian religion with aspects of Pentecostalism.[47]

There is undoubtedly a proliferation of indigenous Chinese Christian churches, about which little is known by the outside world. We know that Pentecostal missionaries from the West were active in China from 1907, but there were only an estimated total of five million Christians in mainland China at the time of the exodus of Western missionaries in 1949, and only a few of these were Pentecostal. Yet the roots of Pentecostal-like Chinese Christianity can be traced as far back as the remarkable 19th-century ministry of Pastor Hsi Shengmo (1835-96) involving exorcism and healing. The greatly influential John Sung (1901-44) would today be regarded as 'Charismatic' and was renowned for his evangelistic and healing ministry.[48]

China today has the largest number of Pentecostal and Charismatic Christians in Asia, and if the most optimistic statistics are true, then possibly the largest in the world. It is extremely difficult to assess church membership in China, especially in the case of movements that remain unrecognised by the government. In 2000, one Chinese house church source put the total number of Christians at around 104 million, but official figures are much lower, admitting to no more than 30 million.[49] Whatever the truth, there has been a remarkable growth of Christianity in China recently, most of which has taken place in unregistered indigenous house churches. There appears to be a proliferation of Pentecostal groups in China at present,[50] a phenomenon quite similar to the spread of Pentecostal-type churches in Africa.

South Korea is a pluralistic society that has been exposed to religious and cultural radiation from the USA.[51] Yet the phenomenal growth of Christianity in

---

46. Johnstone and Mandryk, p. 521; Salazar, p. 194.
47. Jeong Jae Yong, 'Filipino Pentecostal Spirituality: An Investigation into Filipino Indigenous Spirituality and Pentecostalism in the Philippines', ThD thesis, University of Birmingham, 2001, pp. 51, 66.
48. Hwa Yung, 'Pentecostalism'.
49. Lambert, pp. 7-8.
50. Salazar, pp. 79-83.
51. Martin, p. 135.

general and Pentecostalism in particular has taken on a distinctive form in Korea
that is quite different from the forms found in the West. Observers who have
tried to emphasise the 'American' nature of Pentecostalism throughout the world
or the 'Americanization' of Christianity often miss this important fact. Creative
innovations and the selective transformation of 'foreign' symbols are constantly
occurring and, naturally, a synthesising process takes place as new religious forms
interact with older ones.[52]

Protestantism was only introduced to Korea in 1884, and by the year 2000 Protestants formed about 36 percent of the total population, with 55,000 congregations
in 151 denominations.[53] Korean Protestantism has had a history of revivalism,
the most notable being the Wonsan revival of 1903 and the 'Korean Pentecost'
that commenced in Pyongyang in 1907.[54] Preachers whose ministry was accompanied by miracles and healings – especially Presbyterian pastors Kil Sun Joo
and Kim Ik Du, and Methodist minister Yi Yong Do – continued the revival
until the 1930s.[55] The 'prayer mountain movement', also known as the 'Holy
Spirit movement', was a great influence in the Korean church and a pattern for
many to follow. This was clearly a 'Charismatic' movement.[56] The most remarkable growth of classical Pentecostalism took place under the ministry of David
(Paul) Yonggi Cho and his mother-in-law Ja Shil Choi, who began a small tent
church in a slum area of Seoul in 1958 with five members.[57] What became Yoido
Full Gospel Church, reported 700,000 members under 700 pastors in 1993,
making it the largest Christian congregation in the world.[58]

What is certain is that the very nature of Christianity in Asia is changing rapidly,
as it is doing in many other parts of the globe, and that the 'Charismatic face' of
Christianity will continue to play a significant role in the religious world of the
21st century.[59]

---

52. Allan Anderson, 'Pentecostalism in East Asia: Indigenous Oriental Christianity?'. In:
    Pneuma, The Journal for the Society for Pentecostal Studies 22/1 (2000) p. 115.
53. Cox, p. 220; Johnstone and Mandryk, p. 387.
54. Jeong Chong Hee, 'The Formation and Development of Korean Pentecostalism from
    the Viewpoint of a Dynamic Contextual Theology', ThD thesis, University of Bir-
    mingham, 2001, p. 136.
55. Lee Jae Bum, 'Pentecostal Type Distinctives and Korean Protestant Church Growth',
    PhD thesis, Fuller Theological Seminary, 1986, pp. 181-6; Jeong Chong Hee, pp. 161-
    195.
56. Jeong Chong Hee, p. 203.
57. Jeong Chong Hee, pp. 204-6, 208, 218.
58. Cox, p. 221.
59. These and other issues are discussed in Anderson and Tang.

THE CHALLENGE OF PENTECOSTALISM

It is my conviction that Pentecostals in different parts of the world have yet to come to grips with the particular role that the 'freedom in the Spirit' has given them to formulate – often unconsciously – a theology that has meaning for people in different life situations. This is one of the most important features of Pentecostalism, and one that we often overlook. My own work among African Pentecostals has sought to demonstrate that theology is more than written, academic theology; it is also to be found in the preaching, rituals and practices of churches that have contextualized Christianity in such a way as to make it really meaningful to ordinary people. This is 'enacted theology' or 'theology in practice',[60] and it is found in Pentecostalism all over the world.

Pentecostalism challenges older Christian churches as demonstrations of a form of Christianity that appeals to ordinary people, and from which older churches can learn. Pentecostals have a sense of identity as a separated and egalitarian community with democratic access to spiritual power, whose primary purpose is to promote their cause to those outside. These churches see themselves as the 'born again' people of God, with a strong sense of belonging to the community of God's people, those chosen from out of the world to witness to the new life they experience in the power of the Spirit. The cornerstone of their message is this 'born again' conversion experience through repentance of sin and submission to Christ, and this is what identifies them, even to outsiders.

Their many different churches usually emphasize the availability and encourage the practice of gifts of the Holy Spirit by all of their members. The emergence of these churches in the 20th century indicates that there are unresolved questions facing the church, such as the role of 'success' and 'prosperity' in God's economy, enjoying God and his gifts, including healing and material provision, and the holistic dimension of 'salvation'. The 'here-and-now' problems being addressed by Pentecostals in the contemporary world still challenge the church as a whole today. They remind the church of the age-old conviction that for any faith to be relevant and enduring, it must also be experienced. The experience of the power of the Spirit is potentially a unifying factor in a deeply divided church and world; the motivation for social and political engagement; and the catalyst for change in the hope of a new and better world.

---

60. Anderson, *Zion and Pentecost*, p. 2; Anderson, *African Reformation*, p. 217.

2. 'We Shall be Fruitful in this Land': Pentecostal and Charismatic New Mission Churches in Europe

Claudia Währisch-Oblau

For as long as the church has existed, mission and migration have been inseparable. The first church in a Roman city, the first church that was explicitly called 'Christian', namely the church in Antioch, was founded by migrants, or, to be precise, by refugees. In Acts 11.19-26, a paradigmatic description of their spontaneous 'mission from below' can be found. The Gospel is not spread by a strategically planned and theologically reflected mission project, but passed on – more or less accidentally – by untrained believers, without consent or even commission from the 'mother church' in Jerusalem. The mother church only learns of the foundation of a new church after the fact, and reacts with scepticism: Barnabas is sent from Jerusalem to Antioch to evaluate the situation. Only his acknowledgement that, obviously, the Holy Spirit has been at work, enables the Antioch church to become part of the newly forming Christian network.[1]

Such 'spontaneous' forms of mission have not died out with early Christianity. We are confronted with them today, through migration movements from the South to the North, and from the East to the West. Pentecostal and Charismatic migrants see themselves as missionaries within the European context – they will give testimony that God has sent them here with the Gospel, and they start new churches without asking anyone for permission. This is a challenge that has, so far, hardly been understood by European Protestant churches, and is only beginning to enter their reflections about what 'mission' means today.[2] It is therefore

---

1. Barnabas then took the initiative to bring Paul to Antioch, to theologically educate the members of the new congregation. Acts 13 tells us how Paul and Barnabas were later sent out on their first mission journey by the Antioch church. The 'spontaneous' mission preceded the 'planned' mission, and may have even sparked it.
2. Events that have reflected this challenge were the conference 'From Reverse Mission To Common Mission', organized by the United Evangelical Mission (UEM) in May 2000 in Wuppertal, Germany, and a consultation between the then *Samen op Weg-Kerken* (now: Protestantse Kerk in Nederland), the Evangelical Churches in the Rhineland and of Westphalia, and migrant churches, held in Utrecht, the Netherlands, in October 2001. A study process has also been initiated by the Mission in Unity Project of the World Alliance of Reformed Churches. All of these activities have, however, not yet produced any major publications.

high time to take a closer look at the mission work and theology of Pentecostal and Charismatic migrant churches in the European context.

Mission Reversed: An Attempt At A Typology Of 'New Mission Churches'

'All Christian churches and confessions make up the Body of Christ, and our Lord Jesus Christ is the head of these churches. This is why we should skip terms like "foreigners' churches" or "migrant churches", and replace them with "mission churches". They have a task here [in Europe], which is to win new and lost souls for Jesus Christ. If you want, you may call this "mission reversed", for those to whom Christ was once preached have now come back to the areas from which the original preachers set off, to preach Christ in all his goodness to all inhabitants of these areas.'[3] This is how the former Frankfurt pastor and now primate of the Nigerian Church of the Lord (Aladura), Rufus Ositelu, describes the mission of migrant churches in the European context. With this, Ositelu speaks for hundreds or even thousands of African, Asian and Latin American Pentecostal and Charismatic migrant churches which do not see themselves so much as 'diaspora churches', as a 'home away from home' for their members; but rather as part of the outreach movement of the *missio Dei*. That their churches came into being due to migration is just accidental; it does not define them. The real reason for their presence in Europe (or North America, or Russia) is God's mission: They have been sent to preach the Gospel 'to all nations'. They are not just migrants, but 'migrants with a mission'.[4] In principle, therefore, their churches are open to anyone whom they meet, not just for members of their own ethnic, cultural or language group.[5] In consequence, these churches reject the term 'migrant churches',[6] describing themselves instead as 'New Mission Churches'.[7]

---

3. Rufus Ositelu, 'Die Mission der Afrikaner in Deutschland'. Unpublished manuscript of a lecture in Wuppertal, May 16, 2000. Translated from German by the author.
4. I am indebted for this term to Allan Anderson of Birmingham University, who mentioned it in a conversation.
5. Even though, in fact, many may remain monocultural due to language problems. But most anglophone African churches have a substantial number of members from Europe or Asia.
6. Which, in a theological sense, is meaningless anyhow, as the whole church on earth is the migratory people of God (1 Pet 2.11), whose citizenship is with the kingdom of God (Phil 3.20). It is also worth noting that the Greek term *paroikia* has nothing to do with our understanding of 'parochial', but means 'the stay of a non-citizen in a foreign place', or 'the church as a community of such "foreigners"'. In: Walter Bauer, *Wörterbuch zum Neuen Testament* (Berlin, New York: 1971).
7. This term was first coined by representatives of migrant churches at a missiological workshop organized by the United Evangelical Mission in Wuppertal, May 16-18, 2000.

So what kind of churches are these 'New Mission Churches'? First of all, a word of caution: As the situation of the New Mission Churches is extremely fluid, any kind of typology or descriptive pattern has to be used with great caution. It may well be that the ecclesiological categories we have been schooled to think in are a hindrance rather than a help in understanding the changes in the European church scene today. So the typologies and descriptions found below should be understood as preliminary and open to change.

A database of migrant churches is available for the areas covered by the Evangelical Churches of the Rhineland and of Westphalia[8], and is the primary source of data in this paper.

Table 1:   Geographic background of Pentecostal and Charismatic New Mission
           Churches

Of the 393 known migrant churches in the UEM database, 222 may be classified as Pentecostal or Charismatic 'New Mission Churches'.

Geographic area of origin	Number of congregations / churches
Anglophone West Africa (Ghana, Nigeria, Sierra Leone, Liberia, Cameroon)	103
Francophone and Lusophone[9] West and Central Africa (Congo, Angola, Côte d'Ivoire, Cameroon, Togo)	46
Sri Lanka (Tamil)	21
Italy	20
Korea	9
Others	23

8. Set up and maintained by the author for the United Evangelical Mission. A database of African churches in Germany is being established by researchers at the University of Bayreuth within a study project titled 'African Christian movements in Nigeria and Germany between Local Context and Global Influences'. Statistical analysis on migrant churches in the Netherlands has been compiled by Atze van den Broek, 'An Introduction to the 'historical' and 'new' migrant churches in the Netherlands', NZR 034/03 (February 2003).
9. There are very few African Portuguese-speaking congregations. Most Angolans and Guineans attend French-speaking churches.

The membership of these churches varies greatly. Small ones have as few as 20 members, large ones can encompass several hundred adults. The average membership can be assumed at between 50-70 members.

One possibility to distinguish churches is by affiliation: They either see themselves as an independent, non-denominational local church (Independent Local New Mission Churches); as part of a church network founded and headquartered in Europe (New Mission Megachurches, New Mission Church Groups); or as part of a denomination with its headquarters in the country of origin (Denominational New Mission Churches).

Table 2:   New Mission Church congregations by affiliation type: 222 congregations

	Independent Local New Mission Churches	New Mission Megachurches	New Mission Church Groups	Denominational New Mission Churches
African	102	26	7	20
Asian	15	10	4	8
European	3	--	21	--
Latin American	2	--	2	1
Arabic	1	--	--	--
Totals	123 (55%)	36 (16%)	34 (15%)	29 (13%)

Independent Local New Mission Churches[10]: No affiliation

Migrants who come to Europe as Christians and do not find a home in a European congregation, often start a Bible group or prayer cell within their neighborhood or asylum-seeker centre. As such groups grow bigger, they start Sunday worship services and begin to call themselves churches. They are often multiethnic and use either English or French as their language of worship. Some churches also provide regular translations into several languages. Most such churches are pastored by one of the original members who has grown into that role and whom outsiders will call a pastor; almost always a migrant with no close denominational ties. In some cases, such churches are started by an individual

---

10. These churches are mostly of African extraction, but there are also some Asian and Latin American churches among them.

who sees him- or herself[11] called to be a pastor or evangelist. Independent local new mission churches do not always stay independent; some eventually join up with a 'mother church' overseas, or, if they are multi-ethnic, start building more or less formal networks with other, similar churches.[12] Others, set on integration into their European surroundings, join European free churches.[13]

New Mission Megachurches[14]: Affiliation to a strong leader

These churches are still very young, and how stable they will be remains to be seen. They start as non-denominational churches around a charismatic leader – himself[15] a migrant – who eventually attracts a large following. As the church grows, 'satellite churches' are planted, sometimes within the geographic vicinity, sometimes all over Europe and even in the United States. African and Tamil churches in particular have also started a re-reversed mission by planting churches in their country of origin. The headquarters of these churches remain in Europe, and the organization is held together by loyalty to the head pastor rather than by a denominational creed. The head pastor (sometimes called 'bishop', sometimes 'general overseer') tends to rule fairly autocratically and moves around local pastors often, so they cannot establish a local base and become a threat to his authority. Nevertheless, local pastors often strike out on their own after some years of service, usually taking some members with them from the congregation they served.

New Mission Church Groups[16]: Affiliation through language, nationality or creed

Migrants from the same country or ethnic group often have strong informal ties to each other. Therefore, if members of the same ethnic group form churches in different places, they may eventually combine these local churches in an orga-

---

11. Quite a number of these churches are founded and led by women, unlike the other types.
12. See below, New Mission Church Networks.
13. In Germany, many have joined the *Bund freikirchlicher Pfingstgemeinden* (Federation of Free Pentecostal Churches) and some also the *Bund evangelisch-freikirchlicher Gemeinden* (Baptist Convention).
14. Examples taken from the UEM database: Christian Church Outreach Mission (12 congregations in Germany, several congregations in Ghana); Liberty Church International (congregations in Oberhausen, Frankfurt, Kumasi/Ghana, New York/USA). An example with headquarters in the Netherlands is Acts Revival Church (congregations in the Netherlands, Germany, Italy and Greece as well as in Ghana).
15. All of these churches in the UEM sample are led by men.
16. Examples taken from the UEM database: Chiese Cristiane Italiane Nord Europa (Italian Christian Church in Northern Europe), Christ-for-All Evangelistic Ministries.

nized group. Some of these groups only operate nationwide, but many span several European countries, or even include Russia or North America. Such groups may well be understood as denominations in the making, though with strong congregational independence.

These organized groups must be distinguished from looser networks, in which local new mission churches establish contacts with other, similar churches, to share the costs of inviting traveling evangelists and preachers, or jointly organize retreats and revivals.[17]

Denominational New Mission Churches[18]: Affiliation to a 'mother church'

On arrival in Europe, migrants who were members of Pentecostal denominations in their home country, usually first try to join an indigenous congregation. As they often do not feel welcomed there, they look for other migrants with the same or a similar denominational and cultural identity, and then start their own congregation. This happens without any communication with European churches, but often in close contact with the 'mother church'. Once the congregation has stabilized, the mother church is asked to send a pastor or evangelist who is usually financed by the migrant congregation. Only in a few cases do such churches get established by missionaries sent to Europe with the explicit task of planting new churches. This is more common in the case of Korean churches, but rare for African churches, which lack the necessary funds.[19] Such churches usually have a creed and regulated church structures with elected offices, and use Sunday school and worship materials from their home country. It has to be noted, though, that communication with the mother church tends to be sporadic, and efforts to enforce church rules and discipline often end with pastors – and sometimes whole congregations – splitting away.

---

17. For example, the Council of Pentecostal Ministers, a loose network of anglophone African pastors from at least a dozen countries and ethnic groups. This council has, within the last few years, brought its congregations together for all-night prayer meetings, conventions and revivals.
18. Examples taken from the UEM database: Church of the Lord (Aladura), Nigeria; Church of Pentecost, Ghana; Christ Apostolic Church, Nigeria; Redeemed Christian Church of God, Nigeria; Yoido Church, Korea; Assemblies of God, Korea.
19. There are exceptions, though: The Nigerian Redeemed Christian Church of God is known to have commissioned missionaries to Europe, funded by local congregations in Nigeria. But often such funding only covers the first year or so, after which the missionary is supposed to have established a congregation that can take care of his financial needs.

MISSION REVERSED: A CASE STUDY OF LIGHTHOUSE CHRISTIAN FELLOWSHIP

Lighthouse Christian Fellowship (LCF), with its headquarters in Mülheim-on-Ruhr, is a nascent megachurch. Founded by Edmund Sackey-Brown, a Ghanaian pastor with a Baptist background, LCF understands itself as non-denominational, independent and charismatic.

Sackey-Brown, a former Muslim, became a Christian when he was only 14 years old. Expelled from his family, he was able to continue his schooling in a mission school. After studying engineering, he attended a three-year Bible College in Accra. Ordained by the Baptist Convention of Ghana, he started his first church in Accra in the mid-1980s. In 1989, his strongly charismatic congregation decided to send him to Germany as a missionary. For his first years, they raised his salary of 300 German mark (about 150 euro).

Sackey-Brown first came to Aachen, where a pastor friend from Ghana had already started a church that was connected to the local German Baptists. Engaged in street evangelism, he quickly felt that he was unprepared to work in the German context. With the help of some German friends, he attended a six-month course at a German Bible school. He then tried to start a church in Berlin, but with little success. Later, he moved to Mülheim-on-Ruhr, where he started LCF, using rented premises in a small Methodist church.

The first years there were very hard. Money was extremely tight, and the church remained small. By 1998, it had about 100 members. Then, all of a sudden, the church underwent tremendous growth. By the end of 2002, the 400-member congregation had become too large for the Methodist church to accommodate. As none of the other German churches were willing or able to share their premises, LCF rented an old, very ramshackle factory hall close to the railway station. With little money but plenty of enthusiasm, the congregation turned the old building into a church hall that easily seats 600 and which is now almost full on Sundays for worship.

As more and more members were coming to Mülheim from quite a distance, Sackey-Brown started Bible study groups in all of the surrounding towns. Eventually, several of them grew large enough to become 'satellite congregations'. When some members moved to Bielefeld, about 160 kilometers from Mülheim, LCF decided to bring a new pastor from Ghana to start a new congregation there.

The core of the LCF congregations still consists of Ghanaians, but many members also come from other anglophone African countries, as well as the Philippines, Yugoslavia, the Czech Republic and elsewhere. Sackey-Brown makes a conscious effort to reach out to Germans as an evangelist. To further this aim, he closely cooperates with several German Protestant churches. Nevertheless, few Germans have joined LCF to date, even though the new church building in Mülheim offers simultaneous translation via headphones. For Sackey-Brown, cultural differences are to blame for this: 'If I really want to reach out to Germans, I need to shorten the service and also make it less noisy. But then, the Africans will complain.'[20] Realizing that Gospel music is attractive to many Germans, he flew an entire band over from Ghana. Together with LCF's excellent Gospel choir, they perform almost weekly in German churches, at festivals, and sometimes simply out on the street.

Sackey-Brown is himself in great demand as a preacher and evangelist. He speaks at the German Protestant *Kirchentage* as well as in migrant congregations all over the country. He travels abroad as an evangelist, invited through informal Charismatic networks. In 2003, he preached in Nigeria, Suriname and Korea. He used his time in Korea to spend several days to get to know the Yoido Church in Seoul, whose founder, Paul Yonggi Cho, he names as one of his role models.

MISSION REVERSED: ON THE MISSION THEOLOGY OF THE NEW MISSION CHURCHES

The New Mission Churches are an extremely diverse group. But despite their cultural, theological and historical differences, they show a similar practice and theology of mission. Their mission theology, though, is rarely written down.[21] That is why the following chapter makes sparing use of written sources, and mostly relies on many conversations, interviews and observations of the practice of the New Mission Churches.

---

20. Interview, 2003.
21. When New Mission Churches have a written missions policy, as does the Nigerian Redeemed Christian Church of God (RCCG), they usually follow American evangelical or neo-Pentecostal theology, which is often not compatible with their own practice and theology. For example, the RCCG's definition of mission is based on the Lausanne Covenant (1974), which does not even hint at Pentecostal or charismatic theology. The Lausanne Covenant was formulated by the 1974 International Congress on World Evangelization which subsequently sparked the Lausanne Committee for World Evangelization, a world-wide network of Evangelicals.

Mission as Evangelism

As their name implies, mission defined as 'the sending of persons with the Gospel to a people who have not heard at all or heard little in order to make them disciples of Christ'[22], belongs to the core activities of the New Mission Churches. Their 'mission field' is any place 'where the Gospel has not been preached at all (Rom 15.20) and / or where the church available there is dead or not a "Living" Church'[23] – in principle the whole world. Mission is evangelism – and churches which do not practice evangelism are perceived as dead; they need not be taken into consideration.

Where people can be won, new congregations are founded, either in flexible cooperation with local churches which share their practice of evangelism[24], or completely independently. On the one hand, a certain tendency to furthering denominationalism is quite obvious. In the case of the Denominational New Mission Churches, the fulfilling of the evangelism commission is clearly equated with the planting of new denominational churches and the spreading of one's own ecclesiastical scope. Similarly, New Mission Megachurches can be understood as nascent denominations, even though they usually began as being non-denominational. On the other hand, independent non-denominational churches are prone to splits or 'cellular growth': From the first independent non-denominational anglophone African church in Cologne, half a dozen new congregations have come forth, ranging from independent non-denominational groups to congregations that have sought affiliation with Pentecostal churches in Ghana and Nigeria.

The evangelistic zeal of the New Mission Churches is fueled by their expectation of the imminent second coming of Jesus Christ, which is often connected to the evangelical idea that Christ's coming is only possible after the Gospel has been preached to the whole world. As all New Mission Churches share the belief that those who die without having a relationship to Jesus Christ will be condemned to hell forever, the urgency of the evangelism commission is reinforced.[25]

---

22. Missions Policy of the Redeemed Christian Church of God, issued by the governing council of the church, 1-5 Redemption Way, Ebute-Metta, Lagos, Nigeria (April 1999) p. 4.
23. *Ibid.*
24. The stress is on only the practice. Differences in mission theology play a very minor role.
25. Cf. Steven Land, *Pentecostal Spirituality: A Passion for the Kingdom* (Sheffield, Sheffield Academic Press, 1993) pp. 143 ff.

The Power Dimension of Evangelism

While the stress on individual evangelism leads one to place the New Mission Churches within the scope of evangelical tradition, a closer look shows the deep influences of neo-Pentecostal theology. Indeed, evangelism is far more than winning individuals as followers of Jesus Christ. Evangelism is about a power question: Who has power over the world and the people in it – God or God's adversary, the devil and his host of demons? The mission of the church does not simply consist in being the spectator of a cosmic drama – the fight that God has long won – but in being an actor, an instrument used by Christ. 'God is empowering the Church to go to the uttermost parts of the earth to establish the rule and authority of Christ upon the nations.'[26] This is why the church has to practice 'spiritual warfare', which consists mostly of 'aggressive prayer'. In this fight, the church can rely on the power of God; it acts in the name of his authority.[27] Consequently, the evangelistic activities of the New Mission Churches are accompanied by prayer teams which in anglophone African churches are often called 'prayer warriors'. In their everyday practice, prayer meetings in addition to worship services are the most prominent characteristic activity of the New Mission Churches.

The power dimension of evangelism is also tied to the issues of migration. A leaflet produced by Lighthouse Christian Fellowship for an 'International Believers Convention' in 2001, names as its theme 'It's our TIME to possess *our possessions*' [emphases in the original] and adds a Bible verse below: 'For now the Lord hath made room for us in a fertile place with water and trees in the desert and we shall be fruitful in this land!'[28] This theme of taking and possessing the

---

26. Patrick Uponi, 'Possessing the World'. In: *The Catalyst. A Missions Magazine*, published by the Directorate of Missions of the Redeemed Christian Church of God, 1/1, p. 4.
27. These ideas were widely spread by the American theologians, C. Peter Wagner and John Wimber. They shape large parts of the neo-Pentecostal movement and fell on especially fertile ground in Africa and Asia, where they were connected with traditional demonologies. The resulting syntheses have only been researched in some cultures. Cf. C. Peter Wagner, *Engaging the Enemy* (Ventura, CA: Regal Books, 1991); John Wimber and Kevin Springer, *Power Evangelism*, revised edition (New York: 1992); Birgit Meyer, *Translating the Devil. Religion and Modernity among the Ewe in Ghana* (Trenton/ NJ, Asmara/Eritrea: Africa World Press, 1999); Ruth Marshall-Fratani, 'Mediating the Global and Local in Nigerian Pentecostalism'. In: *Journal of Religion in Africa* 28/3 (1998) pp. 278-315.
28. Gen 26.22, where this verse is given as the etymology for the name Rehoboth. The story in this chapter describes a paradigmatic conflict between migrants and indigenous dwellers for scarce resources and obviously speaks to the experiences of black migrants in Europe.

land to which migration or flight has brought one, is a common one, especially in anglophone African New Mission Churches. Their members don't see themselves as exiles bent on return to their home country, but rather identify with the former slaves in Egypt who were brought by God into the promised land.[29] They have a right to be here, even if officials or governments tell them that this is not the case. Consequently, the rejection and racism that they encounter in Europe are seen as signs of demonic dominion over this continent. No African all-night prayer meeting in Germany is complete without an exorcism of the 'territorial demon' of racism from this country.

The militaristic and triumphalistic language of neo-Pentecostal churches often meets with strong criticism from European Protestant churches, especially as the ecumenical understanding of the *missio Dei* was developed as an explicit rejection of triumphalistic and colonial mission concepts. But it is important to pay very careful attention to the speakers and the context. The vocabulary may come from the white American neo-Pentecostal scene,[30] but the speakers here are migrants, people of colour who are marginalized and regularly experience their actual powerlessness. All over Europe, they are daily confronted with individual and institutionalized racism: they have difficulties finding jobs and places to live, and at the aliens' offices they feel helpless against seemingly all-powerful officials. It is the powerless who, putting their faith in God's power, proclaim a reality that contradicts the reality of their experiences.

The 'Materiality' of Salvation[31]

Evangelism that grows out of this power theology and prayer practice is aggressive in so far as it declares the fight against powers that threaten life: Those who are ill are healed in the name of Jesus[32]; victims of violence are assured that God is on their side; those who expect little of themselves are told that God has given them great gifts.[33]

---

29. This may also explain why the New Mission Church do not like to identify themselves as 'diaspora churches'. Rather than crying by the rivers of Babylon in sadness about their lost home, they envision themselves taking over a new land where milk and honey flow.
30. This creates a link between mission and imperialism that must be sharply criticized!
31. Cf. Miroslav Volf, 'Materiality of Salvation: An Investigation in the Soteriologies of Liberation and Pentecostal Theologies'. In: *Journal of Ecumenical Studies* 26/3 (1989) pp. 447-467.
32. Even though Pentecostals and Charismatics know that there is never complete healing for everyone.
33. It is not by accident that the Annual Convention of the Redeemed Christian Church of God consisted of an all-night prayer meeting and a one-day seminar teaching   →

That means: Salvation in the understanding of the New Mission Churches is not just an inner, transcendent occurrence, but a change that encompasses one's material life.[34] This can most clearly be seen in the Pentecostal teaching about divine healing, which has shaped all New Mission Churches: On the one hand, physical healing is understood as encompassed by salvation in Christ, as formulated in Isaiah 53.4-5. On the other hand, healing is possible because Christians in their life on earth already participate in the 'bodily nature of the kingdom of God'.[35]

This is why the evangelistic practice of the New Mission Churches may be called holistic: They are not just interested to 'save souls from eternal damnation', but want people to live a 'life in abundance' (Jn 10.10). Their relationship to Christ will result in everyday miracles: The unemployed find work; migrants receive their residence permit; their children bring home good marks from school; salaries are raised; and racism in the workplace is overcome. It is such miracles that believers report during 'testimony time' in their worship services. Research in Latin America shows that the expectation of such everyday miracles have such an empowering and liberating effect, that poor Pentecostals start to be upwardly mobile in large numbers and even begin to get involved politically.[36] Accordingly, it may be assumed that the theology of the New Mission Churches will help migrants to cope with their everyday problems. However, from observation one can conclude that the New Mission Churches quite often satisfy themselves with the proclamation of God's victory for them. There is plenty of prayer for residence permits and school success, and lots of informal, mutual help, but overall little concerted political or social action.[37] This may be due to the fact that within

---

→ about strengthening one's self-image, networking, education and management techniques. The seminar, titled 'A Date with Destiny', was held June 29, 2002 in Bonn. Also, in sermons, believers will regularly be told: 'God did not bring you to Germany to just clean other people's toilets. He has greater plans for you!'

34. This brings Pentecostal and Charismatic theology into close proximity with Liberation Theology, but clearly distinguishes it from Evangelical beliefs.

35. Earl P. Paulek Jr., *Your Pentecostal Neighbor* (Cleveland TN: 1958) p. 110, quoted according to Volf (note 29).

36. Cf. Richard Shaull, Waldo Cesar, *Pentecostalism and the Future of the Christian Churches: Promises, Limitations, Challenges* (Grand Rapids MI, Cambridge, UK: Eerdmans, 2000); R. Andrew Chestnut, *Born Again in Brazil: The Pentecostal Boom and the Pathogens of Poverty* (Rutgers University Press, 1997); Michael Bergunder, Evangelisches Missionswerk in Deutschland, eds. 'Pfingstbewegung und Basisgemeinden in Lateinamerika'. In: *Weltmission heute* 39 (Hamburg, EMW, 2000).

37. An exception to this observation was the testimony of a Ghanaian medical doctor at New Life Fellowship, Düsseldorf, who had succeeded in opening a private practice after a prolonged struggle. The church had supported him by gathering hundreds of signatures from Africans living in Düsseldorf, demanding that the local chamber of physicians provide a doctor of their own ethnic and cultural background. This support was mentioned during the testimony, but the primary message was: God worked a miracle.

a Pentecostal / Charismatic world-view, material problems often have a spiritual root and therefore have to be solved spiritually. More research is therefore needed to establish whether this theology is actually empowering people to take charge of their life in a foreign land, or whether it merely serves as an opium of the people, a compensation that softens the pain of living on the margins.

PROTESTANT CHURCHES IN EUROPE AND THE NEW MISSION CHURCHES: CONSEQUENCES[38]

Protestant churches in Europe have only started to acknowledge the presence of the New Mission Churches among them.[39] But those churches could contribute a lot to our current discussions about mission and evangelism. Furthermore, their existence means a fundamental challenge for the mission theology and practice of the 'mainline' Protestant churches. I want to briefly sketch two aspects of this challenge:

Mission as Movement: Towards Structural Flexibility

The mission of the migrant churches is characterized by essential unplannedness, decentral organization and apostolic mobility. Evangelism is practiced wherever one just happens to be and to whomever one happens to meet. Church structures and denominational identities are of no importance in facing this great missionary task. Local churches start up spontaneously, grow, split, bring forth daughter churches – and some just disappear again. Ecumenical cooperation does not happen in committees and seminars, but rather in local, concrete, evangelistic activities. Networks develop as they are needed for certain projects, and fall apart as soon as they are no longer needed.

Protestant 'mainline' churches find it hard to enter into dialogue with the New Mission Churches, because they are such fluid and constantly changing entities. It is not surprising that Protestant churches are supporting organizational networks like SKIN[40] in the Netherlands or the Council of African Churches in Ger-

---

38. Some of the ideas in this chapter were first brought up by Dietrich Werner in 'Von missionarischer Abstinenz zur missionarischen Polyphonie in Deutschland: Missionsgeschichtlicher Epochenwechsel, ökumenische Zeitenwende und missionstheologische Schlüsselfragen am Beispiel der Rolle von Gemeinden anderer Sprache und Herkunft'. Unpublished manuscript of a lecture given at the conference 'From Reverse Mission to Common Mission', held May 16-18, 2000 by the United Evangelical Mission in Wuppertal.

39. This is most clearly the case in Italy, where for each Italian-born Protestant there are now two migrant Protestants, most of them either Pentecostal or Charismatic.

40. *Samen Kerk in Nederland* (Together Church in the Netherlands)

many.[41] With this, they want to support the integration of migrant churches into existing structures. But in practice it very quickly becomes clear that neither European parochial and denominational structures, nor mission organizations with their regional and fixed partnership structures, provide an effective structural framework for successful integration.[42]

But could it perhaps be that the flexible organization of the New Mission Churches is much more appropriate to the *missio Dei*, the movement of God's Spirit in the world, than mainline Protestant bureaucratic structures and 'committee culture'? What would happen if the established European Protestant churches were willing, in the course of a dialogue with the New Mission Churches, to radically question their own structures and even reform them? Without doubt, such a process would be painful and difficult. But churches that truly trust in the power of the Holy Spirit should be able to embark on such an undertaking.

Mission as Happening: Towards a Theology of Receiving

Mission in Europe is not the *proprium* of the indigenous, established churches. Nevertheless, as soon as the New Mission Churches break out of their role as clients and receivers of pastoral-diaconal care, they are confronted with state-church-inspired claims of sole representation: 'The European Church is Us!' Whenever estranged nominal members of the 'mainline' Protestant churches discover the living faith and practice of discipleship in a migrant church, accusations of 'sheep-stealing' and 'sectarianism' can soon be heard.[43]

But the presence of the New Mission Churches on European soil is living proof of the fact that mission is not only the task of all churches, but also a happening

---

41. *Rat afrikanischer Kirchen in Deutschland* (RAKD). German Protestant churches have also helped to set up local 'Internationale Konvente' (associations of migrant churches) in Berlin, Frankfurt and Cologne, and the 'Arbeitsgemeinschaft christlicher Migrationskirchen in Nordrhein-Westfalen' (Association of Christian Migrant Churches in Northrhine Westphalia, ACMK). In their founding phase, the day-to-day activities of these associations were administered by Germans. Now that this has changed in many cases, they are usually dominated by Protestant and Orthodox migrant churches, while New Mission Churches play a lesser role.
42. In Germany, for example, only two regional mission organizations (*Evangelisches Missionswerk in Südwestdeutschland* and *Norddeutsche Mission*) have relations with churches in Ghana. Mission organizations like the United Evangelical Mission, therefore find it hard to relate to Ghanaian migrant churches in Germany.
43. In Germany, many 'Sekten- und Weltanschauungsbeauftragte' (church officials, usually pastors, who are mandated to monitor and warn against sects and cults) are strongly and openly critical about New Mission Churches, and often advise Protestant churches against cooperating with them.

with which they are confronted: *Missio Dei*, the working of the Holy Spirit in the world. The European churches, whose missionary theology is shaped by a theology of being sent, need to learn to supplement this with a theology of receiving. Instead of feeling threatened by the New Mission Churches and rejecting their criticism of European 'mainline' Protestantism as fundamentalist and culturally irrelevant, the Protestant churches – now deeply absorbed by their own crises – could, in grateful joy, perceive the work of the Holy Spirit outside the confines of their own organized pastoral activities, and recognize the genesis of new churches and congregations on European soil as 'the grace of God'.[44]

To make this possible, the 'mainline' churches need not just one Barnabas but many: Men and women who are willing to get involved with the New Mission Churches, to get to know them deeply, to ascertain the work of the Holy Spirit within and among them, and to build contacts with the indigenous churches. Where that happens, true partnership in mission can grow between 'historical' Protestant and New Mission Churches, just as it happened all those many years ago between the churches in Antioch and Jerusalem.

---

44. Acts 11.23.

3. Knocking On Heaven's Door: Non-Western Pentecostal Migrant Churches in the Netherlands

Cornelis van der Laan

This paper is a survey of the migrant churches in the Netherlands, in particular the Pentecostal migrant churches from Africa, Asia and Latin America.[1] The focus will be on their relationship with the Dutch churches and society, and some of the missiological questions they raise. We begin by looking at statistics and patterns of immigration in the Netherlands, and then investigate the various migrant churches that developed, and finally consider the relation between the migrant churches with the Dutch churches and society.

IMMIGRATION STATISTICS AND PATTERNS

Looking at the number of inhabitants, the Netherlands is the seventh largest of the 25 member countries of the European Union (EU). Only Germany, the United Kingdom, Italy, France, Spain and Poland have more inhabitants. The population density in the EU averages 116 inhabitants per square kilometre. The population density in the Netherlands is four times this EU average (479), surpassed only by Malta (1,324).[2] The Dutch population has tripled within the span of a century. A hundred years ago, there were five million Netherlanders compared with seven million Belgians. A hundred years later, the Dutch total had increased by eleven million, while the Belgian tally had risen by only three million people.[3] This explains why in the summer you see a mass migration of Dutch cars, caravans and tents heading southwards.[4]

---

1. A previous versions of this paper was presented to the Conference 'Migration und Identität. Pfingstlich-charismatische Gemeinden fremder Sprache und Herkunft in Deutschland', University of Heidelberg, 11-12 June 2004. A German translation is forthcoming. Another version presented to the joint EPTA/EPCRA Conference, Beuggen Castle, Rheinfelden, March 29-April 2, 2005 will be published in the *Journal of the European Pentecostal Theological Association*.
2. *Nederland langs de Europese meetlat* (CBS, 2004) 8.
3. David Coleman and Joop Garssen, 'The Netherlands: paradigm of exception in Western Europe's demography?' In: *Demographic Research* 7/12 (2002) p. 437.
4. *Ibid.*

In 2003, the 16.2 million people that comprised the population of the Nether-lands, included 3 million migrants, of which 1.6 million 'non-Western' and 1.4 million 'Western' migrants.[5] In other words, one in 10 inhabitants is a non-West-ern migrant and a little less than one in 10 a Western migrant. In particular, the non-Western migrants are growing in number. Over the past 30 years the num-ber of migrants has nearly tripled, while the number of non-Western migrants has multiplied tenfold. The population grew during these three decades by a total of three million, half of them being non-Western migrants.[6] Between 1995 and 2003, non-Western migrants were responsible for two-thirds of the population growth. Many migrants live in the larger cities. One-third of the citizens of Am-sterdam are migrants.

The Dutch central statistics office, Statistics Netherlands (CBS), defines all per-sons of whom at least one parent was born abroad as 'allochthonous', meaning foreign-born. One might possess the Dutch nationality and still be categorised as allochthonous in the CBS statistics. In this paper we use the more general term 'migrants', also when citing statistics referring to allochthonous persons. The CBS also distinguishes between Western and non-Western migrants. Because of the presumption that Western migrants are more like the native Dutch ('autochtho-nous'), the CBS decided to also define nationals of Japan and Indonesia as West-ern migrants.

Among the Western migrants, the Germans and persons from the former Dutch Indies or present-day Indonesia are the largest groups. Among the non-Western migrants, the 'classical' or 'old allochthonous' groups are the Turks, Moroccans, Surinamese and Dutch-Antillians. More recently, there have been strong growth rates among other groups. These 'new allochthonous' come from countries such as Iraq, Afghanistan, Iran, China and Somalia. Non-Western migrants form a young age-group: four in 10 'new allochthonous' are younger than 20 years.

Until World War II, migration to the Netherlands was very limited. The first groups of post-war migrants mainly came from the former Dutch colonies in the East: Moluccans (or Ambonese), East-Indies Dutch, East-Indies Chinese and, since 1962, Papuans.

---

5. Centraal Bureau voor de Statistiek (Statistics Netherlands, CBS), internet 2004-05-05. The CBS categorises people from Turkey, Africa, Asia and Latin America as non-Western migrants. People from Japan and Indonesia, however, are categorised as Western migrants, on the basis of their socio-economic and socio-cultural position. This mainly refers to people born in the former Dutch Indies and employees of Japan-ese businesses with their families.
6. CBS, *ibid.*

During the 1960s, many workers from southern Europe arrived: Spaniards, Italians and Yugoslavs (labour migration). Most of them subsequently returned to their home country. Labourers recruited somewhat later from Turkey and Morocco often settled in the Netherlands and had their family members come over (family-reunion migration). Many second-generation Turks and Moroccans still choose their wedding partner from the country of origin (family-forming migration).

People from Suriname and the Netherlands Antilles at first came on a temporary basis as students, but with time decided to stay. Around the time that Suriname gained independence in 1975, a large stream of Surinamese took up permanent residence in the Netherlands.

Until the early 1970s, the Dutch did not think it necessary to reflect on the multi-cultural aspects of their society[7]. Most of the migrants from former colonies were familiar with the Dutch language and culture, while the 'guest-workers' were regarded as being here on a temporary basis. This orderly picture changed in the 1970s. In addition to the groups already mentioned, numerous refugees arrived from Latin America, Asia and Africa (asylum migration), giving rise to a discussion about the new multi-cultural society. Many 'autochthonous' Dutch see their 'allochthonous' fellow citizens as a threat to their own position in the labour and housing markets.

The spectacular growth of asylum seekers in the 1990s, together with developments in the European Union (the Schengen Accord), led to government policy becoming increasingly restrictive. A distinction was made between political and economic refugees. Only political refugees are regarded as 'real refugees'. The government emphasises the social integration of migrants and continues to sharpen the rules for immigration. Several databases with personal information have been connected to enable so-called 'illegals' to be tracked down. Fraudulence of documents was classed a serious crime. With policies such as these, the government is, in fact, encouraging the growth of nationalism and xenophobia.[8]

---

7. Sjaak van 't Kruis, *Geboren in Sion. De relatie tussen de Samen op Weg-kerken, de migrantenkerken en organisaties van christelijke migranten* (Utrecht: LDC, 2001) p. 27.
8. J.A.B. Jongeneel, R. Budiman, J.J. Visser, *Gemeenschapsvorming van Aziatische, Afrikaanse en Midden- en Zuidamerikaanse christenen in Nederland. Een geschiedenis in wording* (Zoetermeer: Boekencentrum, 1996) p. 38.

Migrant Churches

The Dutch central statistics office does not keep records of the religious background of migrants. While ample attention was given to the large numbers of Muslims, it was overlooked that the newer migrants also included many Christians. In 2002, Kathleen Ferrier estimated the migrant Christians to number about 800,000, the majority being Roman Catholic.[9]

In 2003, Atze van den Broek collated data on 343 migrant churches, of which 182 were African. A large number of these churches consist of several congregations or parishes. If these congregations and parishes are included, the total number rises to 624, including 105 Roman Catholic meeting-places. Van den Broek's figures do not include the Dutch-speaking migrant churches, such as many of the Surinamese, Dutch-Antillian and Indonesian churches. Altogether 75 languages were being spoken in the migrant churches.

Roman Catholic migrants form a special group, as they do not form migrant churches. From the point of view that there is only one universal Roman Catholic Church, migrants automatically belong to a local parish. The Roman Catholic Church aims at the integration of all Catholic migrants into the Dutch church. Special parishes for migrants have been established in several cities, but this is seen as a temporary measure.[10] In the larger cities, there are Surinamese and Dutch-Antillian parishes. In Rotterdam, there is a large Portuguese-speaking Cape Verdian parish (5,000 members). There are ethnic parishes (Vietnamese, Indonesian, Japanese, Korean, Sri Lankan, Polish, Croatian and Italian), but also language-based parishes where members of various ethnic groups gather together (English, French, Portuguese and Spanish).[11] These parishes are often led by a foreign priest or a former missionary who speaks the language. Twenty-seven different languages are spoken in the 105 Catholic meeting-places that Van den Broek identified.[12]

Some categorisation can help in identifying the different migrant churches, not including the Roman Catholic migrant parishes. For the German situation, Claudia Währisch-Oblau suggested four different types:

---

9. Kathleen Ferrier, *Migrantenkerken. Om vertrouwen en aanvaarding.* In the 'Wegwijs' series (Kampen: Kok, 2002) p. 30.
10. Kruis, p. 29. Ferrier, *Migrantenkerken,* 30-31. Judith Maaskant, *Afrikaan en Katholiek in Rotterdam: waar kerk je dan?* (Nijmegen: Katholieke Universiteit, 1999).
11. Jongeneel, pp. 44-49.
12. Atze van den Broek, *An introduction to the historical and new migrant churches in the Netherlands* (February 2003). Unpublished hand-out during the symposium on non-Western Pentecostalism in the Netherlands (Amsterdam: February 2003).

1. Established/denominational congregations
2. Traditional missionary/denominational congregations
3. Reverse missionary/denominational congregations
4. Independent missionary/non-denominational congregations[13]

For the Dutch situation, the migrant churches can best be first divided in historical migrant churches and the newer migrant churches.

HISTORICAL MIGRANT CHURCHES

Most of the members of the 'historical' migrant churches come from countries with historical ties to the Netherlands, mostly former colonies. These are the churches from Indonesia, the Moluccas, Suriname and the Dutch Antilles. Their members are familiar with the Dutch language and culture.

Some of the historical migrant churches declare solidarity with the newer migrant churches. The *L'Eglise Wallone* (Walloon Church) has existed in the Netherlands for more than 400 years, but maintained the French language and culture as the Walloon section of the Netherlands Reformed Church. Nowadays the Walloon Church feels it may be able to assist the French-speaking migrant churches.[14]

Indonesian and Moluccan churches

Some 290,000 migrants came from the Dutch East Indies between 1946 and 1958. They were of Dutch origin, of mixed Dutch-Indonesian origin, Chinese or Moluccan and, from 1962 onwards, also Papuan. Except for the Moluccans, their integration in Dutch society went rather smoothly. Many were Protestant and became members of the Dutch Reformed Church. Others joined the Roman Catholic Church or Pentecostal churches. The Indonesian Christian Association (*Persekutuan Kristen Indonesia di Nederland*, PERKI), which by then was already in existence, developed into an ecumenical fellowship that cherishes the Indonesian heritage. Although not a church, it organises bilingual church services in five cities. The Indonesia Dutch Christian Church (*Gereja Kristen Indonesia Nederland*, GKIN), was established in 1985. Initially a Chinese church, GKIN developed into a multiracial church. The church belongs to the Reformed tradition. Regular church services are held at eight locations. The GKIN tallies 600 registered members.

---

13. Claudia Währisch-Oblau, 'From Reverse to Common Mission ... We Hope'. In: *International Review of Mission* 89/354 (2000), pp. 467-83. The article refers to Protestant migrant churches in the Rhine-Ruhr region in Germany.
14. Ferrier, *Migrantenkerken*, p. 36.

The Moluccan community comprised 4,000 military men and their families. Their stay in the Netherlands was supposed to be temporary. Integration into Dutch society was not encouraged. Other than the Indonesian Christians, the Moluccan Christians (90 percent were Protestant) did not join the Dutch Reformed Church. The Moluccan Evangelical Church (*Geredja Indjili Maluku*, GIM) was founded in 1952, after the request to be an overseas branch of the Moluccan Protestant Church was turned down by the mother church.[15] It was only after violent actions such as the train hijacking in the late 1970s by young Moluccan radicals, that the Dutch Protestant churches started to dialogue with the GIM. In the 1990s, the GIM established official ties with the mother church. The GIM has 65 congregations and 25,000 members.

There are at least 17 other groups of Moluccan churches in the Netherlands. Altogether, the Moluccan Protestant churches have 35,000 members. Since 1999, there have been outbreaks of violence between Muslims and Christians on Ambon. Organisations for humanitarian aid have been founded by Moluccans in the Netherlands, in which Muslim, Roman Catholic and Protestant communities work together.

Pentecostal Indonesians

Among the migrants from the Dutch Indies were also Pentecostal believers. Rather than joining the existing Pentecostal assemblies, these believers often preferred to form their own congregations. Five national bodies developed:
1. *Christelijke Gemeenschap De Pinksterbeweging* (Christian Fellowship The Pentecostal Movement), related to the mother church in Indonesia, *Gereja Gerakan Pentekosta*.
2. Bethel Pentecostal Temple Fellowship Netherlands, affiliated to the mother church, Bethel Pentecostal Temple, in Seattle (USA) and in contacts with the *Gereja Pentekosta di Indonesia*.
3. Bethel Pentecostal Church Netherlands has branches in Ghana, Nigeria, Zambia and the Philippines.
4. Bethel Fellowship Netherlands.
5. *Volle Evangelie Bethel Kerk* (Full Gospel Bethel Church). Following the example of the mother church in Indonesia (*Gereja Bethel Indonesia*), the church affiliated with the Church of God, Cleveland (USA).

---

15. The Moluccans in the Netherlands supported the South Moluccan Republic, while the Moluccan Protestant Church supported the Indonesian Republic. The separation from the mother church was a bitter experience. Ferrier, *Migrantenkerken*, p. 55.

In addition to these five national bodies with worship services in Dutch, a number of independent Pentecostal churches with bilingual services were founded. An example of the latter is the *Gereja Kristen Perjanjian Baru Air Hidup* (Christian Church of the New Covenant Living Water), founded by John Tan in 1991, with congregations in Zwolle, Amsterdam and Rotterdam. Altogether, there are about 50 Pentecostal Indonesian congregations totalling 6,000 members.

Surinamese and Dutch-Antillian churches

Of the nearly 320,000 Surinamese in the Netherlands (compared with 450,000 in Suriname!), one might expect – given the statistical ratios in Suriname – 80,000 to be Protestant and another 74,000 to be Roman Catholic. The actual numbers that attend Reformed or Catholic churches are much smaller. The Surinamese theologian Hesdie Zamuël explains that 'this country does not stimulate you to go to a church'.[16] The Surinamese do not like 'boring' services, therefore they would rather join the singing *Evangelische Broedergemeente* (Moravian Church) or the Pentecostal churches. The Moravian Church used to be a very small church in the Netherlands, but was the largest Protestant church in Suriname. With the immigration from Suriname, the church has seen spectacular growth and a transformation from being a white church to a predominately non-white church. Most of the 15,000 registered members in seven congregations are from Suriname. This church became one of the initiators to form a national platform for migrant churches.

Many other Surinamese joined existing Pentecostal churches or formed new Pentecostal churches. The largest Pentecostal church in the country, Maranatha Ministries in Amsterdam, consists mainly of Surinamese and Dutch-Antillians. However, its pastor, Stanley Hofwijks, does not want his church to be labelled as an migrant church.

NEWER MIGRANT CHURCHES

The members of the many 'new' migrant churches established during the past two decades, come from all over the world. The growth of these churches is spectacular. Their members are usually not (yet) familiar with the Dutch language and culture.

---

16. Hesdie Zamuël, 'Dit land stimuleert je niet om naar de kerk te gaan'. In: *Wereld en Zending* 22/2 (1993) p. 28.

The grouping of these churches follows Ferrier's categorisation of three types[17] to which is added a fourth type and resembles the categories of Währisch-Oblau referred to earlier:

Ecumenical mainstream migrant churches

Migrant churches belonging to one of the mainstreams of the ecumenical churches. The churches in the Orthodox tradition – Russian, Serbian, Greek, Syrian and Ethiopian Orthodox, Armenian Apostolic – and churches in the Protestant tradition, like the Scots International Church. Some of these churches were founded in cooperation or in consent with the Dutch churches and aim at a specific group, such as the Norwegian and Finnish seamen's churches in Rotterdam. Members of these churches usually have a legal status. The pastors have an academic training, are fully accepted by their Dutch colleges, and have no problem in acquiring a work permit.

Reverse-mission migrant churches

Migrant churches related to a mother church in the country of origin. These churches are the result of missionary activities from the country of origin to the West, with their own international network. They usually have no ties with ecumenical networks in the Netherlands and are therefore little known here. African examples are the Kimbanguist Church, The Church of Pentecost, Resurrection Power and Living Bread Ministries. Asian examples include several Korean churches as the result of missionary activities from Korea, and the Japanese Christian Fellowship Church. The members of these churches vary from middle-class workers to labourers and asylum-seekers. The pastors often do not speak Dutch and may have problems with work permits.

Independent migrant churches

Migrant churches founded by migrants as an independent church, usually started by a charismatic leader. These churches have little financial stability. The pastors generally lack formal theological education. Many have experienced a calling from God and some attended a Bible College for a few months. Obtaining a

---

17. Ferrier, *Migrantenkerken*, pp. 37-39. Afe Adogame comes to three types of African religious groups in Europe: 1. Branches of mother churches with headquarters in Africa; 2. Churches with headquarters in Europe, but with intension to open branches in Africa and elsewhere; 3. Inter-denominational groups or para-church organizations. Afe Adogame, 'The Quest for Space in the Global Spiritual Marketplace. African Religions in Europe'. In: *International Review of Mission* 89 (2000) p. 400.

working permit is difficult. Examples of these churches are The Everlasting Salvation Ministries, The House of Fellowship International, The Acts Revival Church International, The True Teachings of Christ Temple.[18] These churches often have an international network of their own. If they grow, they start daughter churches in other cities as well as in neighbouring countries and sometimes even in the country of origin. In this phase they often expand their name with signifiers like International, Worldwide or Global. From this point on they might also be considered a denominational church.

These churches often split, but this is not always seen as negative. For African Christians, a split can also be seen as a sign of power and growth.[19] Independent churches vary strongly in membership. Many find it important to be registered at the Chamber of Commerce, which provides them a certain status.

Denominational migrant churches

Independent migrant churches that have developed into a denomination of their own, but also migrant churches that from the start are member of a denomination akin to the one in the country of origin. A good example is the Assemblies of God. A number of migrants from Africa and Latin American belonged to the Assemblies of God. In the Netherlands they founded an Assemblies of God migrant church. They are member of the Dutch sister-denomination and often keep ties with the Assemblies of God in the country of origin as well as with the Assemblies of God in the USA. Examples are El Elcuentro Con Dios, Covenant World International Ministries, Glad Tidings Assemblies of God. The Dutch Verenigde Pinkster- en Evangeliegemeenten (United Pentecostal and Gospel Assemblies) affiliated with the Assemblies of God, formed a special international district to facilitate all the migrant churches.

Except for the first type, probably all these churches are non-Western, among which the African churches form an important category. Most of the churches of the second type and nearly all of the third and fourth type are Pentecostal, Charismatic or Spiritual churches. These churches have a strong missionary zeal to evangelise also outside their own language or culture. Although they try to be missionaries to the native Dutch, the latter do not respond to their evangelistic efforts. Many of the church members are asylum-seekers, refugees without a legal status or economic migrants. If they are employed, they have the so-called Three-D Jobs: Dirty, Difficult and Dangerous.[20]

---

18. Ferrier, *Migrantenkerken*, pp. 39-41.
19. Ferrier, *Migrantenkerken*, p. 39.
20. Ferrier, *Migrantenkerken*, p. 40.

Missionary activities of migrant churches

In an article on the mission of migrant churches in Europe, missiologist Jan Jongeneel points out that not all migrant churches are missionary active.[21] At least
two groups give no priority to missionary activities. Firstly the migrant churches
originating from Muslim or communist countries with no religious freedom. Primary they want to continue the church life of their mother country. Sometimes
these believers are afraid that missionary activities in Europe might have reper-
cussions for family members at home. They know that the secret services of their
mother country are also present in Europe. The second group is formed by Christians from strongly secularised non-western countries like Uruguay and Singa-
pore. Just as the mainline European churches they accept secularisation as a fact.
Therefore they rather develop a strategy for survival than a missionary program.
The majority of the migrant churches are however missionary active. For a number of them the missionary activity is limited to the own language or culture
group, while others consciously try to convert the secularised West. In this so-
called reversed mission the African Christians take the lead.[22]

CHRISTIAN MIGRANTS IN RELATION TO DUTCH CHURCHES AND SOCIETY

The established churches at first paid no attention to the newer migrant Christians, expecting them to join the existing churches without any fuss. As already
mentioned, the Roman Catholic Church set up some special parishes for
migrants.[23] But it is only in the last decade that the Dutch churches have gradually become aware of the migrant churches.

On the initiative of the Hendrik Kraemer Institute, the first conference of representatives of non-Western migrant churches was held in Oegstgeest in November
1992. This saw the launch of the Platform of Non-indigenous Churches (*Platform
van niet-inheemse kerken*). It also led to the publication, in 1996, of an extensive
survey of the migrant churches.[24] An updated survey of migrant churches by
Kathleen Ferrier, the then co-ordinator of SKIN, was published in 2002.[25]

---

21. Jan A.B. Jongeneel, 'De missie van migrantenkerken in Europa' *Wereld en Zending*
    33/4 (2004), p. 63-69.
22. Jongeneel, 'Missie', p. 69.
23. Kruis, p. 29.
24. J.A.B. Jongeneel, R. Budiman, J.J. Visser, *Gemeenschapsvorming van Aziatische,
    Afrikaanse en Midden- en Zuidamerikaanse christenen in Nederland. Een geschiedenis
    in wording* (Zoetermeer: Boekencentrum, 1996).
25. Kathleen Ferrier, *Migrantenkerken. Om vertrouwen en aanvaarding*. In the 'Wegwijs'
    series (Kampen: Kok, 2002).

SKIN

The name of the Platform of Non-indigenous Churches was officially changed in 1997 to become SKIN, the acronym of *'Samen Kerk in Nederland'* (Together Church in the Netherlands). The play on the English word 'skin' was felt to be relevant, since the colour of our skin still in part determines our position in society. The mission of SKIN is for migrant churches to co-operate together, to fully be a church – each in their own fashion – in the Dutch society. In particular, the migrant churches were looking for practical help in finding locations for worship, becoming registered and getting to know the rules and laws of Dutch society. SKIN is sponsored by the Protestant Church in the Netherlands and has become the most visible representative of the migrant churches and organisations. The 54 member churches and organisations currently represent 65,000 members.

Other bodies of newer migrant churches are GATE (Gift from Africa to Europe), which is associated with the Alliance of Evangelical Churches in Africa and the Council of Pentecostal Churches, based in Amsterdam.

Dutch church involvement in the newer migrant churches

The Dutch pastor of the Presbyterian Church of Ghana, Atze van den Broek, has since 1989 been pastor to refugees on behalf of the Council of Churches in Amsterdam. He maintains a national database of places of worship, languages and numbers of migrant churches.

Cura Migratorum coordinates the migrant parishes in the Roman Catholic Church. The Foundation Support Fund for Allochthonous Churches (*Stichting Ondersteuningsfonds Allochtone Kerken*, SOFAK) is a charity that provides small grants to migrant pastors and churches. The foundation GAVE (Gift) links migrants, shortly after their arrival in the country, with the Dutch churches. The Protestant Church in the Netherlands appointed Sjaak van 't Kruis as staff coordinator for the migrant churches in its national secretariat in Utrecht.

The Centre for Education and Faith (better known as *De Schinkel*) of the Protestant Congregation of Amsterdam helps the city's migrant churches with Dutch language classes and finding rooms or buildings for church activities. They also organise excursions to migrant churches.

There are 170 migrant churches in Amsterdam, about half of them in the Bijlmer suburb. Accommodation is a big problem. An inventory resulted in a list of 130 migrant churches looking for rooms and only 34 available locations[26]. When the Bijlmer was designed 40 years ago, there was felt to be no need for any church buildings. The two purpose-built centres that have since been constructed are being used at full capacity. Some churches are located in multi-storey car parks, which charge high rents. A project launched in May 2004 aims to raise seven million euro to build three multiplex church centres in the Bijlmer, to accommodate 45 migrant churches.[27]

Dutch society and the newer migrant churches

In a study of the relationship between the Protestant Church in the Netherlands and the migrant churches, Sjaak van 't Kruis is of the opinion that the multicultural society does not exists. He views the Dutch society rather as a multi-ethnic society, in which the various groups live in separate compartments. Van 't Kruis points out that the migrants themselves, for reasons of sheer survival in Dutch society, remain within their own ethnic group. But he also draws attention to a trait of Dutch society that prefers compartmentalisation. Van 't Kruis concludes that 'up till now the word "multicultural" has only referred to the presence of a variety of cultures without there being any trace of togetherness'.[28] According to Jos de Beus, professor of social science, the so-called tolerance of Dutch society is in fact indifference, as displayed in remarks such as 'I approve of all life-styles, so long as they don't cause me any trouble'.[29] Gerrie ter Haar, professor of social studies, once observed it was no coincidence that 'apartheid' is a Dutch word.[30]

Kathleen Ferrier, former co-ordinator of SKIN, regards this lack of interest in the other as a major problem. She refers to the shadow side of secularisation. Holland is one of the most secularised countries in Western Europe. Religion has all but disappeared from public life. By contrast, migrants hold religion to be of great importance in their daily life. Ferrier stated that 'by not acknowledging the social significance of religion, the government falls short, hinders integration; we remain living alongside one another, and the suspicion among us grows'.[31]

According to Patrick Kalilombe, migrants often come with unrealistic expectations.[32] Africans assume that the hospitality they know is a universal custom.

26. Erika Feenstra, 'Kerken (z)onder dak'. In: *Kerkinformatie* (September 2003).
27. 'Bijlmerkerk: geef ze de ruimte', Stichting [charitable foundation] De Bijlmerkerk, www.bijlmerkerk.nl.
28. Kruis, p. 27.
29. *Ibid.*
30. Katheen Ferrier, 'Religie in ontwikkeling', lecture for Cordaid, January 16, 2002.
31. *Ibid.*
32. Patrick Kalilombe, 'De Afrikaanse diaspora in Europa: een persoonlijke beschouwing'. In: *Wereld en Zending* 21/3 (1992) pp. 71-79.

When they come to Europe, they expect a warm reception and special attention, just as the whites received when they visited Africa. Instead, they soon learn that they are seen as impostors, against whom all precursors are acceptable. The rich West is a hard world for outsiders. It is a fight for the survival of the fittest.

Young Africans view Europe as the land of milk and honey. They say to themselves: 'Years ago the white man came as an economic migrant to Africa and other places, and now it is our turn to go to their country.'[33] They sell all they have to buy a plane ticket, only to have their dream shattered when the immigration officers at the Western airports interrogate them. The prison in Alkmaar is one place where many 'illegal migrants' spent their last day in the Netherlands. On one of the prison walls is written 'The Boulevard of Broken Dreams'.

How the undocumented live in fear and uncertainty is illustrated by the following quote: 'If we go into town, we have nothing that betrays our identity. We have become a walking encyclopaedia of telephone numbers, addresses and other personal data of ourselves and of others. Because that is what the police is looking for when they stop us.'[34]

The migrant churches provide a social network for the migrants in need. Among the members there any many without official documents who receive help from the church. For this social function see the article 'Co-Partners in one Mission' in this book.

CONCLUSION

Just as in neighbouring Germany, Belgium, Britain and nearby France, migrant churches, many of them Pentecostal, are also present in the Netherlands. They display significant growth and vitality, especially in the larger cities. Many of their members live here without a proper legal status, because we collectively decided to lock our European Union doors to the migrants from beyond our borders.

Migrants often come with dreams of finding green pastures and a land of milk and honey. While they become disappointed in their expectations of finding a material heaven in our part of the world, they do find a home in the migrant

---

33. J. Amoako-Aduesei, 'Droombreuk. Een rapportage over Afrikanen in Amsterdam'. In: *Wereld en Zending* 22/2 (1993) pp. 13-20. 'Working in the Boulevard of Broken Dreams' is the title of a report that Father J. Amoaka-Aduesei wrote about the activities of the Roman Catholic chaplaincy for Africans in Amsterdam.
34. Amoako-Adusei, p. 17.

churches. These are places of belonging, islands of hope in the midst of a harsh, secularised Western world.

Deprived of access to proper housing, labour, medical care and social security, the undocumented cry out to God for their needs. They know from experience that it is better to trust in God than in Western society. So they keep on knocking at heaven's door.

4. Pentecost Behind the Dykes: Diversity and Recent Developments in the Pentecostalism Movement in the Netherlands

Huibert Zegwaart

The Pentecostal movement is a relatively small and rather fragmented section of the Christian Church in the Netherlands. This article offers a survey of the various strands of Dutch Pentecostalism. Following a short introduction, the first section provides a brief description of the various Pentecostal entities or denominations. The second section contains an analysis and prognosis of some tendencies within the Pentecostal movement, together with some personal comments.[1]

INTRODUCTION

The Pentecostal movement is reputed to be one of the more dynamic sections of the Church in the Netherlands.[2] It is active and there are often developments, positive or otherwise, that occur within and through the movement. Examples include the emergence of a major new denomination and the founding of several new congregations. Then there is the merger of the two largest Pentecostal denominations. Other developments worth mentioning can also readily be found, such as the astonishing growth of non-Western Pentecostalism and the growing rapprochement between Pentecostals and ecumenicals. On the other hand, it would also be easy to draw up a list of events that have caused scandals (such as church splits) or controversies (for example, due to dubious practices). All these underline that Dutch Pentecostalism is both multifarious and vibrant.

---

1. Two disclaimers have to be made from the outset. The first concerns objectivity. It should be clear that the writer has been an active participant in the recent history of Dutch. Pentecostalism. Nevertheless, a conscious attempt to be fair and objective in describing the varieties of Dutch Pentecostalism has been undertaken. The reader will be the judge of the writer's objectivity. The space and scope of this chapter are also limiting factors for a complete treatment. The view of one single author is, of course, necessarily limited.
2. The dynamism of the Pentecostal movement was acknowledged by C. van der Laan and P.N. van der Laan, in the title of their history of the Pentecostal movement in the Netherlands and Flanders: *Pinksteren in beweging* (Kampen: Kok, 1982).

The diversity of the movement may to a considerable degree be attributed to its international orientation. It is this particular trait that gives cause for hope about the possible integration of the migrant churches with the indigenous movement in the near future.

VARIETY AND NUMERAL STRENGTH OF DUTCH PENTECOSTALISM

Cees van der Laan has provided a concise and useful overview of the history of the Pentecostal movement in the Netherlands in the *New International Dictionary of Pentecostal and Charismatic Movements*.[3] There is therefore no need to repeat this here.

To outsiders, the Pentecostal movement in the Netherlands can appear to be a confusing *mêlée* of independent churches, denominations, and church-like organisations. It is difficult to chart the somewhat complicated connections between all these bodies. Moreover, it is also hard to give an estimate of how many adherents the Dutch movement has, since many groups do not keep reliable records. However, those figures that are available point to significant changes that have occurred over the past 15 years. Since the survey conducted by Van der Laan in 1989, several groups have declined drastically or even ceased to exist, while others have experienced considerable growth and new groups have come into being. My aim here is to highlight the dynamism of the movement by drawing on Van der Laan's surveys (1989 and 1996) and the statistics he provides, as the basis for my analysis.

The total membership of Pentecostal groups in the Netherlands in 2004 is estimated to be somewhere between 100,000 and 115,000 persons. Assuming this estimate to be reliable, permit me some observations and a few comments. Firstly, the uncertainty as to the precise number of adherents has been taken into account by allowing for a wide margin of error of 15,000. Secondly, the 2004 estimate implies considerable numerical growth when compared with the estimated figures of Van der Laan, who reported some 70,000 adherents in 1989 and 80,000

---

3. In S.M. Burgess and E.M. van der Maas (eds.), *New International Dictionary of Pentecostal and Charismatic Movements* (Grand Rapids: Zondervan, 2002). The title is abbreviated elsewhere as *NIDPCM*. Older surveys by the same author are: 'Wegwijzer voor de Nederlandse pinksterbeweging'. In: C. van der Laan (red.), *Pinksteren* , vol. 20 of *Religieuze bewegingen in Nederland* (Amsterdam: VU, 1990) pp. 127-130; and 'De Pinksterbeweging in Nederland'. In: *Kerk en Theologie* 47/4 (October 1996) pp. 285-298.

in 1996. Thirdly, these figures are of the total membership (including children) of the more than 650 Pentecostal congregations.

The estimates do not include those adherents who belong to the Charismatic movement. Nor do the estimates cover the vast majority of so-called 'migrant churches' that sprang up in the late 1980s and '90s. The reasons for these exclusions should be obvious. Charismatic believers are included in the statistics of the denominations to which they belong. As for the migrant churches, is very difficult to obtain precise information about them, since they are very much independent and only some of these churches seek to relate to their indigenous counterparts. One cannot be sure about the numbers of people involved in such ethnic churches, but conservative estimates would put them at several tens of thousands.[4]

In trying to determine the total number of Pentecostals, Charismatics and neo-Pentecostals in the Netherlands, a figure of 200,000 would probably not be far off the mark. This is equivalent to about 1.25 percent of the 16 million population in the Netherlands.[5]

PENTECOSTAL DENOMINATIONS

Of the various denominations, the *Verenigde Pinkster- en Evangeliegemeenten* (Assemblies of God in the Netherlands, VPE) is by far the largest. Paradoxically, it is both the youngest and also the one with the longest history. The reason for this lies in the VPE being the result of a merger in 2002 between the *Broederschap van Pinkstergemeenten* (Brotherhood of Pentecostal Churches, BPG) and the *Volle Evangelie Gemeenten Nederland* (Full Gospel Churches in the Netherlands, VEGN). Yet the historical roots of the BPG reach back to the arrival of Pentecostalism in the Netherlands, in 1907. In previous surveys, they were clearly the two largest Pentecostal bodies.

---

4. Amsterdam Southeast houses over 80 migrant churches, of which the vast majority belong to the Pentecostal movement. Although most of these churches are rather small, others have memberships of over 500 persons.
5. Compare the 1,040,000 for the renewal given in the *NIDPCM*, p. 184. Note that the figures given for the Netherlands are highly inaccurate: the number of 52,390 for classical Pentecostals suggests a precision that cannot be attained, and is moreover way beside the mark. The figure given for the number of Charismatics (537,922) is most definitely wrong. In so far as there are any figures available, they point to a constituency of around 12,000. As for the number of neo-Charismatics (the figure of 449,668 cited in *NIDPCM* is puzzling to Dutch researchers), nothing can be said any more certainty than that it must run into the tens of thousands.

In 1989, the BPG reported that it comprised 45 congregations. By 1996, this had grown to 61, only to drop to 57 in 1998.[6] The number of adherents increased from 7,000 (1989) to 11,000 (1996), but then dropped to 10,500 (1998). Part of the decline was due to the fact that some small congregations had disbanded, while several congregations with little active involvement in the Brotherhood were asked to reconsider their membership, which in a few cases led to their ending their affiliation with the denomination. The figures for 1998 also involved a change in the way of calculating. The total numbers of adherents recorded in previous surveys included the membership of some 20 congregations whose pastors held ministerial credentials with the BPG, but whose church was not affiliated with the denomination. There was therefore an indirect connection with these churches. If the figures of the 1998 survey were adjusted accordingly, then the BPG's growth would clearly be seen to have been considerable. The main contributing factor for the denomination's growth was the affiliation of independent churches, in addition to the denomination founding a few new churches.

More important than the numerical strength is the character of the BPG as a pragmatic fellowship of congregations and ministers. Until 1966, the BPG was a loose fellowship of Pentecostal ministers. Officially they were the representatives of their congregations, but in reality they did not act as representative voices of their churches. In 1966, the BPG entered into a formal relationship with the Assemblies of God (USA). The American denomination insisted that the BPG reorganise itself to become a body in which the congregations have a real say in the affairs of the Brotherhood. Further, they counselled that the BPG adopt a doctrinal confession. This led to the formulation of the *'Fundamentele Waarheden'* (Fundamental Truths). At the same time, the *Centrale Pinkster Bijbelschool* (Central Pentecostal Bible School; now Azusa Theological Seminary) and Teen Challenge were founded. In the years that followed, other initiatives were adopted that gradually transformed the nature of the BPG fellowship.

The VEGN, the partner that merged with the BPG, went through a different process of development. In 1989, there were 44 congregations with a total membership of 8,400 persons. By 1996, the numbers had declined to 37 and 5,000 respectively. Two years later, they grew again, to 38 congregations with some 8,000 members. The decline in the early 1990s was largely due to a number of churches in Flanders choosing to affiliate with the *Verbond van Vlaamse Pinkstergemeenten* (Federation of Flemish Pentecostal Churches, founded in

---

6. In that year, the present author conducted a survey in preparation for his 'Pinkster-kerken in Nederland. Een culturele lappendeken'. In: *Parakleet, Kaderblad voor geestelijk werkers* 67 pp. 3-7 and 68 pp. 3-10. *Parakleet* is the official periodical of the United Pentecostal and Evangelical Congregations in the Netherlands (VPE).

1992). Some churches became independent, while others went over to the newly-formed *Bereagemeenschap* (Berea movement). Other churches joined the VEGN during this period, but this could not compensate for the loss of membership through secession. The sudden increase in total membership between 1996 and 1998 was due to a change in the way of counting: the VEGN began to also include younger children in its statistics. This resulted in a considerable increase in the number of members, even though the number of congregations increased by only one. The VEGN's organisational structure remained rather minimal. It maintained its character as a loose fellowship of congregational leadership that met twice a year.

The VEGN has been the catalyst in unifying several Pentecostal groups. In the 1980s, its officers approached the leadership of the BPG with the request that the two boards come together for prayer and contemplation. The initiative was gradually broadened to include board members of other Pentecostal bodies. Thus, the *landelijk gebedsplatform* (national prayer platform) was born, which became the forerunner of the *Landelijk Platform van de Pinkster- en Volle Evangelie-beweging in Nederland* (National Platform of the Pentecostal and Full Gospel Movement in the Netherlands; hereafter referred to as the National Platform), founded in 1994. With hindsight, their initiative was a first step toward the VEGN-BPG merger and the consequent formation of the VPE. In many respects, the VPE resembles the structure of the former BPG, while in other respects it brought about innovations. As it was with both the BPG and the VEGN, the VPE retains a congregational structure of governance. At the interdenominational level, the VPE participates in such bodies as the *Interkerkelijk overleg inzake de Overheid* (Inter-Church Council on Government Affairs) and the *Raad voor Contact en Overleg inzake de Bijbel* (Council for Contact and Consultation on the Bible). It is also the only Pentecostal denomination that has a government-recognised, fully accredited theological seminary. The school, Azusa Theological Seminary, was affiliated with the Free University of Amsterdam in 2002.

One further aspect that needs to be mentioned here is the numerical size of the VPE. At present, this runs to 116 member churches and around 16,500 adherents. The number of affiliated ministers who are full and personal members exceeds 175.[7]

Of all the Pentecostal groups, *Kracht van Omhoog* (Power from Above, KvO) is perhaps the most controversial. Its name is derived from the magazine published under that name from 1936 until 1993. *Kracht van Omhoog* dates back to the

---

7. Figures date from 2003.

early 1960s and reached its peak in the late 1970s and early '80s. The movement, which never became a formalised denomination, is best described as a group of local congregations that identified themselves with the teaching espoused in the magazine. In the 1960s, *Kracht van Omhoog*'s editor, the legendary Jo van den Brink, began to teach a doctrine that turned out to be highly divisive. His teaching held that whoever commits sin does so under the influence of a demon. Accordingly, demons were cast out of believers. Older Pentecostal churches denounced the new doctrine as heretical. In reaction, Van den Brink began to rethink Christian theology in the light of his fundamental conviction. He then rejected the doctrine of original sin and developed a method of biblical interpretation that was highly allegorical. His doctrine became known as 'the high road'.

The decline of this movement set in soon after Van den Brink died in 1989. Some eight years earlier, he had placed the editorship of *Kracht van Omhoog* in the hands of his son-in-law, Peter Bronsveld, who was a more irenic writer. Toward the end of his life, Van den Brink actually hinted that he had at times gone too far with his insights. Under his leadership, the movement had been quite isolated. But Bronsveld sought to make contact with other Pentecostal groups. While he succeeded and the movement was admitted to the national prayer platform (around 1990), not all adherents were happy with the new course. Some congregations wanted to cling to the Van den Brink doctrine and develop it even further.[8]

When Jo van den Brink died in 1989, there were still 37 congregations totalling some 6,000 adherents that viewed the movement favourably. But four years later, the constituency had shrunk to the extent that the magazine could no longer be published. After it ceased to appear in 1993, the number of *Kracht van Omhoog* congregations dwindled to a mere 13 in 2002 and no more than 1,500 adherents.

The *Rafaël Gemeenschap Nederland* (Rafael Fellowship, now Foursquare Netherlands) started in the 1980s. It comprises 39 congregations and outposts, and about 3,000 adult members.[9] The growth of this group can be attributed to several causes. For one, church planting was an avowed policy objective of this newly-formed denomination. Further, several independent congregations joined, as did

---

8. A new periodical was started, named *Studieblad*, in which J.G. Bulthuis and C. Visser propagated some 'new insights' that ultimately led to division within the '*Kracht van Omhoog*' churches. Bulthuis and Visser no longer regarded Jesus as a divine person and taught that the Holy Spirit is an unlimited power rather than a person. This clearly went beyond Van den Brink's views.
9. In 1989, Van der Laan counted only nine congregations. By 1998, the number had risen to 28 (including outreaches). Total membership in 1989 was slightly over 1,000 persons, and about 2,500 in 1998.

some other congregations that decided to switch their previous allegiances and join *Rafaël Nederland*. In 1987, *Rafaël* became part of the International Church of the Four Square Gospel. In doctrine, *Rafaël* falls within the mainstream of Pentecostalism, but in matters of polity the denomination is more hierarchical than the denominations and movements discussed so far. In 1996, the church published a Dutch translation of *Foundations of Pentecostal Theology* by Guy Duffield and Nathanael van Cleave. In 2000, it opened a theological training school in Amersfoort. *Rafaël Nederland* is a founder-member of the National Platform.

The organisation *Johan Maasbach Wereld Zending* (Johan Maasbach World Mission) is named after its evangelist-founder. Maasbach, whose preaching activities began in the early 1950s, founded the organisation in the wake of the legendary campaign by the American healing evangelist Tommy Lee Osborn, in 1958. The campaign, in which Maasbach served as interpreter, drew nationwide interest, a fact that was unprecedented in Dutch history. Maasbach continued to preach the 'Full Gospel' message that focused on the possibility of healing through faith in God. Judged by the content of his preaching and the type of spirituality he promoted, Maasbach must be situated within the mainstream of Dutch Pentecostalism. However, because of the methods he used, most Pentecostal groups did not want to be associated with his organisation. Moreover, many Pentecostal leaders objected to the authority structure in his organisation, especially since power was concentrated in his own family. This remained so even after Maasbach's death in 1997.

By 1996, the number of adherents had dropped from 3,600 members (in 1989) to a mere 2,500 in 12 assemblies.[10] In the interval, the organisation went through considerable upheaval caused, among other, by the exodus of a number of co-workers led by Jan Zijlstra, who established his own work in the vicinity of Leiden. A number of former associates also brought several charges against Maasbach that led to preliminary investigations by the civil authorities. These investigations, however, yielded nothing to warrant legal proceedings against the evangelist. After the commotion had subsided and Maasbach's death, there was relative peace in its ministry. At present, there are 11 congregations and a membership of not more than 4,000 persons.[11]

10. According to David Maasbach, this figure was too low (telephone conversation on May 11, 1998).
11. However, in view of the number of subscribers to *Nieuw Leven*, the organisation's monthly, it may be surmised that the number of sympathisers must be larger than the figure cited here. Yet, since it is likely that they belong to other denominations, they are not included in our count.

The work started by evangelist Zijlstra, who broke with Maasbach, is based in nearby Leiderdorp. Zijlstra is seen conducting healing campaigns throughout the country. These campaigns are organised together with local Pentecostal churches.

The *Bereagemeenschap* (Berea Movement) was officially founded in 1997, preceded by some years of preparation. This accounts for the fact that one year after it was established there were already 30 congregations with a total membership of over 3,000 persons. Present figures show it has grown to 38 churches with around 5,500 members. The form of organisation is kept rather simple, since it continues in the tradition of facilitating 'fellowship' between the leadership of the member churches. The matrix of this community is first of all to be sought in circles of *Kracht van Omhoog*. In 1992, Rob Allart, the central figure of the movement, took the initiative of establishing an interdenominational organisation called *Vriendschap Geestelijke Leiders* (Amity network of religious leaders). A number of the pastors who belonged to this circle (but not all of them) joined the new denomination. In many Berea churches, phenomena associated with the so-called 'Toronto blessing' can be found. The conviction and emphasis that believers, despite their new birth in Christ, can be under the influence of evil spirits is a common conviction in Berea churches. Individual believers have to be cleansed from the influence of evil spirits. The denomination joined the National Platform in 1998.

In the wake of the Toronto blessing, the 'new' type of spirituality found a home in several independent churches. Some of these changed their name to include the epithet Capitol Worship Center and placed themselves under the apostolic ministry of a South-African 'prophet' named Ashley McGuicken. They consider themselves to be a part of the 'New Wine' movement, identifying themselves with internationally renowned evangelists like Benny Hinn and Rodney Howard Browne. There are also connections with the so-called 'Word of Faith' Movement, founded by Kenneth Hagin. The movement may be described as 'left-wing Charismatic', indicating a type of spirituality that seems to attribute less authority to the Scriptures than to immediate religious experience. A characteristic of these churches is the predilection for the five-fold ministry. Appealing to Ephesians 4.11, they hold that all five ministries mentioned should be in evidence in every congregation. The ministry of prophet is especially valued.

Not many churches in the Netherlands have associated themselves with this movement. In 1998, there were seven and, two years later, eight. The number of adherents lies somewhere between 900 and 1,000. Yet, from the fact that a full-colour magazine, *Charisma*, has been published and a yearly conference, 'Euro Spirit', is being organised with speakers from abroad, one may surmise that the number of sympathisers must be wider.

Evangeliegemeente 'De Deur' ('The Door' Gospel Church) is the Dutch branch of the Christian Fellowship Churches (also known as the New Harvest Churches) founded by Wayman Mitchell in Prescott, Arizona. This group asserts that Christianity, including the traditional Pentecostal churches, has divorced itself from the New Testament Church. The Dutch branch was founded in 1978. Two years later, Rudy van Diermen became its leader and remained the undisputed leader for almost 20 years.

In 1989, there were about 500 members in nine churches and outreaches. The figures were considerably higher in 1998: thirty-three churches and about 1,250 adherents. In 2003, the group claimed that the work comprised 43 churches and outreaches with around 2,500 adherents. In view of the internal problems that have pervaded in the church, these figures appear to be rather high.

'Het Keerpunt' Verenigde Pinkstergemeente ('Turning Point' United Pentecostal Church) has very few adherents but represents a stream of Pentecostalism that is often overlooked, to wit 'Oneness Pentecostalism'. A characteristic of the movement is its denial of the Trinity. Founded in the Netherlands in 1986, this missionary outreach of the 'International United Pentecostal Church' consists of five small congregations comprising no more than 170 adult believers. Since the rest of Dutch Pentecostalism is thoroughly Trinitarian in doctrinal outlook, there is no contact with this group.

Originally, *Victory Outreach* was solely concerned with evangelising troubled youth and young adults. The organisation developed programmes to break drug addiction and to help people rebuild their lives. Since their purpose was to confront needs that were hardly met in regular churches, they decided to start congregations in the major cities where these needs were prevalent. This happened in 1985, when the congregation in Amsterdam was started as an experimental effort. To date, there are eight Victory Outreach churches throughout the country. What distinguishes them from regular Pentecostal churches is the stress on discipleship and on developing discipline. Hence, the church is organised with a structure that is more hierarchical than is usually found in the Dutch context. The group joined the National Platform in 2002. Victory Outreach has a membership of around 1,500 persons.

A very recent group is *New Frontiers International* (NFI), which was begun in the United Kingdom. The movement's central figure is the Reverend Terry Virgo of Brighton, whose writings on church life betray a staunchly restorationist view: the church has strayed and must be restored in its original power and holiness. This requires that the five-fold ministry be rediscovered and re-instated. In the

Netherlands there are five churches. The number of adherents probably does not exceed 1,000.

The *Bethel Pentecostal Churches* were founded by repatriates from the Dutch colonies in South-East Asia in the 1950s. They therefore occupy a unique position within Dutch Pentecostalism. Apart from the fact that many of these rather small denominations carry the word 'Bethel' in their name, their membership largely consists of Dutch people who are partially or completely Indonesian. Some of these groups are struggling to maintain their numerical strength. Their success in this regard seems to be relative to the extent that they have effectively adapted to the dominant culture of their new home country. Within the last decade, a number of the Bethel communities have been able to overcome their isolated position. The National Platform has been helpful in this regard.

The *Volle Evangelie Bethel Kerk* (Full Gospel Bethel Church) currently has nine congregations with over 500 'friends', compared with 16 churches and 2,600 'friends' in 1989. This denomination, which was founded in 1975, has always sought contact with Pentecostal denominations with a more indigenous background and was a co-founder of the National Platform.

The *Bethel Pentecostal Temple Fellowship Nederland*, founded by C.J.H. Theijs in 1960, is a small denomination with eight churches and a total membership of about 330 persons. The fellowship joined the National Platform in 1995.

Bethel Fellowship Nederland was formed in 1980 after some congregations broke away from the Bethel Pentecostal Temple. There are five congregations with a total membership of about 250 persons.

Bethel Pinksterkerk Nederland (Bethel Pentecostal Church) was founded by C. Totaijs in 1963. At present there are 16 congregations with a total membership of 3,500 persons. Perhaps this group was the most isolated of the Bethel denominations. Part of their doctrine was based on divine revelations received by F.G. van Gessel in 1935. He taught that there were several types of Christians, most of whom were only admitted into the other courts of the (spiritually perceived) Temple. Christians who had received the baptism with the Holy Spirit, were allowed into the holy section, and only those who were ready for the rapture were Christians of the Holy of Holiest (in effect, those belonging to the Bethel Pentecostal Church). This doctrine entailed an elitism and exclusivity that prevented co-operation and fellowship with other Pentecostal denominations until the end of the century. It was only in the year 2000 that they applied for membership of the National Platform.

Christelijke gemeenschap 'de Pinksterbeweging' (Christian Fellowship of 'the Pentecostal Movement') is a Pentecostal group that came into being in 1953. There are only three churches with a total membership of about 270 persons.

Of the roughly 650 congregations within the Pentecostal and Full Gospel movements, less than half are linked with a central organisation. The rest are independent churches. Some local Pentecostal groups comprise more than a single congregation. In and around The Hague the *Morgenstond* (Morning Hour) churches formed a rather homogeneous grouping until about a decade ago.

Maranatha Ministries was founded as a local Pentecostal church around 1960. The church began to attract people from different ethnic backgrounds in the early 1980s. It is currently a church characterised by an impressive ethnic diversity. Though most members are Netherlanders of Surinamese origin or immigrants from the Dutch Antilles, other adherents are from more than 25 nationalities. The church has seven congregations in and around Amsterdam. They include an English-speaking congregation largely consisting of African immigrants in the suburb Amsterdam South-East, also known as the Bijlmer. The church's membership exceeds 2,700 persons.

SOME OBSERVATIONS

Much has happened within Dutch Pentecostalism during the last 15 years. A few observations are in order here: Firstly, there is the emergence of some new denominations, that results in a further fragmentation of an already fragmented movement. Secondly, the growth of the Pentecostal movement in the Netherlands appears to have slowed down in comparison to the tremendous growth in the 1980s, a view shared by several observers. In this, the Dutch movement follows the tendency of Pentecostalism worldwide. Yet, this does not mean that growth has halted altogether. In fact, Pentecostal churches have experienced growth and development in a period when most churches in the Netherlands are struggling to maintain their numerical strength. This is, however, no reason for triumphalism, since Pentecostal growth lags behind that of the Dutch population as a whole.

The tendency in Dutch Pentecostalism to fragment is not a source of joy for those who value ecumenism. What could be a flourishing of different types of spirituality within the Pentecostal body, often turns out to be a source of division. Protagonists and antagonists usually appeal to the same Scriptures, but to different passages. This is often done without much regard for proper exegesis or hermeneutical methodology. More often than not, the search for texts that serve as proof occurs when the joy is great at having discovered new religious truth or undergone some religious experience. Conversely, the antagonists 'roam' through the Old and New Testaments in the heat of the argument. Such a situation is hardly conducive to fruitful theological reflection.

Another tendency that gives little cause for joy, is the preference of many local congregations to remain independent. This preference probably stems from an anti-institutional sentiment that is also prevalent in other religious circles in the Netherlands. The decision to remain independent is often motivated by apprehension of 'outside interference in internal affairs'. There is also an economic motive: the fear that affiliation will involve unnecessary expenses and administrative hassles. These motives obscure the benefits that can be derived from membership within a larger body. Granted, in many cases these benefits are not as tangible as the monthly contribution that the congregations pays, but they involve interdependence, solidarity and mutual aid, cross-fertilisation and realisation of projects at a level that transcends the local church. Often, it is hard to convince people that these benefits outweigh the perceived drawbacks. This is especially the case with large churches and those that are flourishing. When one is riding on the crest of success, it is easy to overlook the need for co-operation. This ultimately leads to a spirit of autarchy, self-sufficiency and isolationism, which in time could turn into sectarianism.

NATIONAL PLATFORM

Another significant trend within Dutch Pentecostalism is also evident. There is a new tendency to neither highlight the differences between the various Pentecostal movements, nor to question the good will of the other. Instead, Pentecostals have begun to talk to each other in a context that is not governed by controversy and strife. There is, then, a growing 'ecumenism of the heart' within the Dutch Pentecostal movement. Moreover, this trend has found concrete form in 1994 with the setting up of the National Platform of the Pentecostal and Full Gospel Movement in the Netherlands. After the decision to formally establish the National Platform was made, its realisation followed rather quickly. This was possible because a simple organisational structure was adopted in which only denominations could become members. The term of office was limited to two years, and it was agreed that both of the officers could not be from the same denomination. The constitution was also quite limited in scope. Once formed, the organisation then obtained a broadcasting licence from the government. In 1996, the organisation invited some members of parliament to discuss ethical issues of concern to Christians with a more conservative outlook.

Only time will tell as to which of the two following tendencies will become dominant within Dutch Pentecostalism: one in which Pentecost behind the dykes will remain separated from each other by newly-dug canals; or the other, whereby efforts to unify result in bridges being built across the demarcation lines. Of course, it is a beautiful sight to behold straight canals cut though the green fields. Yet, the Lord's prayer of John 17 is compelling: 'That they may be one.' Of heart? Yes! But, by the same token, also in visible unity!

5. INTERMEZZO – Called to be 'Refugee Missionaries': The House of Fellowship in Amsterdam

Cornelis van der Laan

This article gives a portrait of Tom Marfo and The House of Fellowship, which he founded and of which he is the pastor, in the Bijlmer suburb of Amsterdam. It illustrates the social function of the migrant churches in Dutch society and gives us an interesting missiological perspective.

> The Sunday service starts at three o'clock in the afternoon. The meeting-place in Amsterdam Bijlmer is not easy to find, hidden in a desolated parking garage that is about to be torn down. I am late, but that does not seem to worry anyone.

> The House of Fellowship is a migrant church. Most members come from Nigeria and other African countries. Services last three hours and are held in English. The average age of the 200 participants is young. The members are well dressed, some in traditional clothing. Music is loud and lively, people are dancing.

> After one hour of singing, Pastor Tom Marfo preaches for one hour. He reads from 2 Kings 4 the story of Elisha and the Shunammite woman. In his inspiring sermon, he emphasises the importance of hospitality and relates this to the situation of the migrants in the Netherlands. After the sermon, a baby is dedicated to God. The whole extended family comes forward.

> After prayer and blessing, the parents receive a document signed by the pastor sitting behind a table. This part of the service is rather official. I realise that most of the members have no legal status, so the document becomes highly significant. The church is the place where all people have a status, where they are restored in dignity.

> After the ceremony there is time for prayer and more singing. For the offering, all members go forward in dancing. Finally there are some announcements. I am warmly welcomed as a guest and called forward to greet the

assembly. Afterwards people stay for drinks and to meet one another. Certainly this is a house of fellowship.[1]

Justice Tom Marfo, founder of The House of Fellowship, was born in Ghana on Independence Day, March 6, 1957.[2] His entire family was Muslim. His father was head imam of the village where Marfo grew up. Missionaries from the Methodist Presbyterian Church came and founded the only school in the village. Thus Marfo came to accept the Christian faith:

> If the mission and the mission schools had not been there, I had not known God and I had not enjoyed an education ... I want to do something in return for the good the missionaries have done.[3]

To further his education, Marfo went to the secondary school of the Catholic Mission in Accra. A goat was sold to pay for his expenses. After high school, he became involved in Pentecostal circles and active in youth work and mission. He received in-service training with the African Christian Mission (ACM) and was sent as a missionary to Nigeria in 1980. Four years later, he was sent to England to study theology, but he studied marketing instead. He prospered and bought a house in London. But his spiritual life suffered. An illness caused him to rededicate his life to God and return to Ghana in 1989. Back in Ghana he worked with the Christian Medical Mission Resource Foundation, an offshoot of the ACM. In 1992, he founded the Rural Soul Winning Evangelistic Ministries International (Rusowem) to send out missionaries to the rural areas of the Ashanti region in Ghana.

In 1993, Marfo was assigned by the ACM to pastor an ACM church in Portland, Oregon, USA. On his way, he stayed with a nephew in Amsterdam, where the American Embassy refused him a visa for the USA. Looking for a new direction, he felt called to remain in the Netherlands:

> I saw girls from Africa on the streets selling their body. I started to investigate. They all appeared to be here as sex-slaves. As property of criminals they were sold to others. They were treated worse than animals. They did not dare to go to the police, because they had no papers. Therefore I started a campaign against this modern form of slavery.[4]

---

1. C. van der Laan, Visit to the House of Fellowship, Amsterdam, February 2004.
2. Tom Marfo, interview of June 30, 2004, Amsterdam. Cf. 'Nederland is harde grond'. In: *Nederlands Dagblad* (September 9, 2002).
3. Guido de Bruin, 'Nederland zal fout van ongeloof inzien'. In: *Nederlands Dagblad* (July 6, 2001).
4. Reina Wiskerke, 'Voorganger in de Bijlmer'. In: *Nederlands Dagblad* (March 12, 2004).

Marfo noticed that Africans did not feel at home in the Dutch churches, so he started prayer meetings. About the cool reception he received from the local churches at Amsterdam, he said:

> When we as Christians came to the Netherlands, we expected a welcome committee of the local churches. Instead we received a diplomatic welcome during a business meeting. We have found out that the Dutch way of fellowship is in reality rather remote.[5]

African migrant churches were being set up. To bring more unity among these churches, Marfo founded the Pentecostal Council of Churches, in 1995. Two years later, he established the church The House of Fellowship and the Christian Aid and Resources Foundation, a charity to rescue African women forced into prostitution. Together with the church, the foundation runs eight apartments in the Bijlmer, where these women receive housing. Over the past years, 350 women were rescued and given help to find a respectable place in society.[6] For his achievements, Marfo received the Marga Klompe Award in 2002 and the 'Hero of Amsterdam' municipal award in 2003.

The social function of the church is clear. People who are in need expect help from the church, even if they do not go to church. The pastor is daily confronted with the problems of the migrants: suicide, mental problems, no residence permit, no working permit, and no money to buy food. Churches are the most important places to find hope. For migrants, the church is their home. Many of the homeless sleep there. It is also their restaurant, where the poor receive their daily bread.

Most of the members of the House of Fellowship are 'undocumented'. Marfo refuses to use the term 'illegal', for no creature of God can be illegal. The term illegal dehumanizes and stigmatizes the undocumented as criminals. 'It is not a crime to be illegal.' Many without jobs are helped by the church to find work, sometimes so-called black jobs because they lack proper permits. When someone finds a job, the members rejoice; 'we beat the drums', says Marfo, just as when someone finds an unused bus ticket.[7]

---

5. 'Migrantenkerken dagen gevestigd christendom uit'. In: *Nederlands Dagblad* (February 28, 2003).
6. Maarten Vermeulen, 'Jonge asielzoekers prooi voor loverboys'. In: *Nederlands Dagblad* (January 14, 2004).
7. Nynke Dijkstra and Wout van Laar, 'Verslag van een kennismaking met The House of Fellowship, Amsterdam Zuidoost' (NZR-November 2002).

The church provides computer and language classes, which are subsidised by government institutions. The church takes obvious pleasure in the fact that the government unwittingly subsidises the education of the undocumented! About 70 percent of the members of The House of Fellowship are Nigerian, five percent Ghanaian and 25 percent come from other (West) African nations.

Marfo is a board member of SKIN, the national platform of migrant churches, and also founder of the Pentecostal Council of Churches Amsterdam Southeast (PCC). About 20 churches participate in the council, the majority being African. In 2000, the council was supported by lawyers in deeming as unjust the government's policy on verifying Ghanaian identity papers. A government circular in 1996 'blacklisted five countries as having a notorious record concerning the production of fraudulent identity documents. At the top of this list was Ghana followed by Nigeria, India, Pakistan and the Dominican Republic'.[8] In practice, it means that the identity of a document-holder has to be verified by an investigation in the country of origin. These measures are felt to be insulting and 'a blow to the Ghanaian dignity and self-esteem'.

In the monthly all-night prayer meetings, African Christian migrants ask God to remove the allergy of the Dutch against the gospel. Marfo challenges the Dutch government to investigate the economic advantages of the so-called illegals:

> Look on the metro station early morning; those on their way to clean the offices are nearly all black. They like to work, even though they earn in black money much less than others in the Netherlands. They like to work overtime, for then they have money for their relatives and they can save for their future.[9]

The only way to stop the stream of immigration is economic justice. Marfo points to the African dictators who have stolen billions of dollars and placed them in secret bank accounts in the West. The American secret service knew where to find the accounts of Al Qaeda in 24 hours. 'Why is not everything done to trace our stolen money? Instead we can pay interest for 300 years on the money we were allowed to borrow from the West.'[10]

Marfo fights against the materialism, individualism and selfishness of Dutch society. He finds it 'heartbreaking' to see the nation turned away from the herita-

8. Rijk van Dijk, 'Ghanaian churches in the Netherlands'. In: I. van Kessel (ed.), *Merchants, Missionaries & Migrants: 300 years of Dutch-Ghanaian Relations* (Amsterdam: KIT, 2002) p. 89.
9. Reina Wiskerke, 'Voorganger in de Bijlmer'. In: *Nederlands Dagblad* (March 12, 2004).
10. Wiskerke.

ge of their forefathers, the missionaries who brought the gospel to other continents. He criticizes the Dutch churches for no longer acting as the 'moral compass' of the nation.

In the Missionary Quarterly Council (*Missionair Kwartaalberaad*), a national platform for dialogue between missionary organizations and Pentecostals, Marfo formulated the mission of the migrant churches to the Netherlands:

> I believe that the Lord sent us here, legally and illegally, to be co-partners with you in the one mission of God; to assist each other in our common calling; that is to create healing places in the broken-ness of our societies.[11]

Migrant churches feel they have something valuable to contribute to church and society in the Netherlands. These 'refugee missionaries' may be materially poor, but they bring with them their 'rich faith, which they have acquired by experience in their daily dependence upon God for their survival'.[12] Fortunately, contacts between the indigenous and migrant churches are developing albeit slowly. There is much that both sides have to offer and to receive, to share and to learn from each other.

---

11. Nynke Dijkstra and Wout van Laar, 'Verslag van een kennismaking met The House of Fellowship, Amsterdam Zuidoost' (NZR-November 2002).
12. Tom Marfo, 'Reverse Mission: The Emerge of the Migrant Churches and their Impact on the Dutch Society', Paper presented to the Missionary Quarterly Council (*Missionair Kwartaalberaad*) in 2002.

II   DIALOGUE

6.   'Pentecostals-Ecumenicals Dialogue'[1]

Huibert van Beek

It has often been said that future church historians will describe the 20th century as the century of the modern ecumenical movement. The starting-point is commonly seen to have been the World Mission Conference at Edinburgh in 1910, and one could point to the Joint Declaration on the Doctrine of Justification between the Roman Catholic Church and the Lutheran World Federation in 1999 as a worthy milestone at the opposite end of that time-span. The foundation of the World Council of Churches in 1948 and the Second Vatican Council in 1962-65 will for sure be engraved in church history.

During the past one hundred years, the ecumenical movement has deeply marked the churches and has had a lasting impact on their relationships with one another, their theology, their liturgy, their mission, service and witness to the world. Some would go as far as to say that it is indeed the single most important phenomenon in Christianity, in what Hobsbawm has characterised as the 'Age of Extremes'.[2] To paraphrase Hobsbawm's metaphor, the churches have moved from the extreme of ignoring each other at the start of the century, to the embrace of recognition and agreement at its close.

ONE CENTURY, TWO MOVEMENTS

Yet to single out one characteristic of any time of history, whether secular or ecclesial, brings with it the risk of being blind to other aspects. It often matters from which point the observer views the past. For anyone for whom the ecumenical movement is the determining factor of modern church history, there is little reason to look beyond its horizon. However, that effort is required to discover

---

1. This title – in somewhat clumsy English – is taken from a banner that marked a remarkable event in Seoul, Korea, in November 2002. At the invitation of the International Theological Institute of the Yoido Full Gospel Church, members of the WCC-Pentecostal Joint Consultative Group engaged in a dialogue on globalisation with staff of the Institute. The meeting was attended by over 300 Pentecostal pastors and students of the Korean Assemblies of God, of which the Yoido Full Gospel Church is a part.
2. *Age of Extremes: The Short Twentieth Century*, Eric J. Hobsbawm, Penguin 1994. As a matter of fact, Hobsbawm does not mention the ecumenical movement at all and hardly speaks of the churches, except to mention their declining influence in society.

that the 20th century has in fact been marked not by one, but by two movements that have shaken the churches: Ecumenical, for sure, and Pentecostal.

While in mission and oikoumene circles minds are getting geared towards the centenary celebration of Edinburgh 1910, another commemoration is just around the corner, largely unnoticed by the tenants of ecumenism: the celebration of Azusa 1906. The revival which took place that year in the church of Rev. William Seymour on Azusa Street in Los Angeles, is widely considered to be the beginning of the Pentecostal movement (although another theory dates it back to around 1900, at the Bible School of Charles Parham in Topeka, Kansas). From there, the experience of 'Spirit Baptism' began to spread rapidly across the territory of the United States and beyond, and the growth of the movement has been exponential, especially since the second half of the 20th century.

Today, the number of Pentecostal and Charismatic Christians is estimated at more than 500 million.[3] In terms of the magnitude of the movement, its vitality and ongoing expansion, it is not exaggerated to say that the burst of Pentecostalism is an unprecedented phenomenon in the history of Christianity. It is particularly successful in the global South, in Latin America, the Caribbean and Africa; but also in Asia, and among the immigrant communities from these regions in Europe and North America. There is growing evidence that the movement emerged simultaneously at several points of the globe, around the time of the Azusa Street Revival and independently of the presence of American missionaries.

One century, two movements, each have taken separate courses, away from each other and largely ignoring one another. That is an amazing – and humbling – reality of our recent history as churches and Christians. It is all the more so because each one claims to be the fruit of the Spirit. The ecumenical movement would simply not be able to understand itself, if it did not believe that the extraordinary renewal it has witnessed in so many churches and among so many Christians, is the work of the Holy Spirit. Even a staunch Evangelical or Pentecostal critic of ecumenism does not have the right to deny that. The Pentecostal movement is by its very nature Spirit-driven. No Christian who has been reared and nurtured ecumenically is allowed to cast doubt on that. Could it be that the Holy Spirit has moved in such apparently confusing ways in the 20th century that we, at the dawn of the 21st, are left with a seemingly insoluble division in Christianity?

---

3. According to David Barrett, *World Christian Encyclopedia*, (Oxford, University Press, 2001).

At the risk of disappointing the reader, this article is not the place to go into a theological debate on the workings of the Holy Spirit. But it is certainly appropriate to underline here the crucial importance of such a reflection for any rapprochement between the two movements. Some Pentecostal scholars and scholars of Pentecostalism would argue that Pentecostalism was in fact intrinsically ecumenical at the time of its inception.[4] The Azusa Street Revival was an invitation to join and taste the blessed unity of Spirit-filled believers, regardless of denomination, race or social status. It was indeed little less than a miracle that in 1906 Los Angeles black and white Christians from various denominations were together experiencing the same baptism in the Spirit.

Here is some sound theological ground to build a concept of unity that does not get bogged down in disentangling doctrinal obstacles but could open a window to an 'Ecumenism of the heart' (a *cri de cœur* sometimes heard in WCC circles). A.J. Tomlinson, a founding father of the Church of God[5], says in one of his writings that Christians could be truly one if they put obedience to the commandments of Jesus above all creeds, dogmas, doctrines and traditions.

A similar, pragmatic understanding of ecumenism is at work in the Charismatic movement, which transcends confessional barriers while at the same time respecting the integrity of each denomination and avoiding the setting up of new churches. In Pentecostal circles it is sometimes called the ecumenism of the Spirit. Whether or not it is a valid option, or at least offers a basis for serious theological discussion, remains an open question. The problem is that, on the one hand, the ecumenical movement is unaware of Pentecostal scholarship and, on the other hand, most Pentecostal leaders do not seem to be interested in an ecumenical dialogue.

SOME CROSSING-POINTS

The qualification that the two movements in the 20th century have 'largely' ignored each other, is on purpose. Although few in number and of limited impact, there have been instances of contact and co-operation that could have provided a different impulse to the course of events. The Assemblies of God, the largest white Pentecostal denomination in the USA, has since 1921 been a member of the International Missionary Council, through the Foreign Missions Conference

---

4. For example, Cecil M. Robeck, Professor of Church History and Ecumenics at Fuller Theological Society; Walter Hollenweger, author of the standard work *The Pentecostals* (1972); and others.
5. Known as the Church of God (Cleveland) to distinguish it from other denominations with the same name.

of North America. When, in 1950, the latter became the Department of Foreign Missions of the National Council of Churches of Christ in the USA, the Assemblies of God chose to stay, although the denomination did not join the NCCC.

In the years after the Second World War, the Assemblies of God were associated with Church World Service and indirectly involved in programmes of interchurch aid in Europe coordinated by the WCC. From the early 1950s until the late 1970s, Rev. David du Plessis, a visionary Pentecostal ecumenical pioneer laboured to bring Pentecostals into dialogue with the World Council of Churches and the Roman Catholic Church. He was at the International Missionary Conference in Willingen in 1952, where he met for the first time the General Secretary of the WCC, W.A. Visser 't Hooft, and attended all the WCC Assemblies from Evanston (1954) to Vancouver (1983).

Du Plessis was originally from the Apostolic Faith Mission in South Africa. From 1947, when the Pentecostal World Conference[6] was founded (in Zürich, Switzerland), he functioned as the secretary of this body. The PWC was formed 'to demonstrate to the world the essential unity of Spirit-baptised believers, fulfilling the prayer of the Lord Jesus Christ 'that all may be one' (John 17.21). Its main activity was the convening of a large international gathering of Pentecostals every three years. This international ministry led David du Plessis to join the American Assemblies of God, in 1955. His ecumenical efforts resulted eventually in the Roman Catholic-Pentecostal Dialogue, which officially started in 1972 (and is still continuing).

With the World Council of Churches nothing tangible happened, in spite of Du Plessis' presence at assemblies and other meetings. How to explain this remains an open question. The difference may have been that, on the Roman Catholic side, Du Plessis found an ally in the person of Killian McDonnell, a scholar of the Charismatic renewal movement, whose support in bringing the dialogue into being was crucial.

The modest ecumenical openings of the Assemblies of God came to a halt in the first half of the 1960s, when a conservative leadership took over and the denomination was the target of the anti-WCC fundamentalist Carl McIntire of the International Council of Christian Churches. The co-operation and relationships with the NCCC were discontinued and David du Plessis was disciplined with the withdrawal of his credentials. (He was reinstated as an ordained minister in 1980).

---

6. Now called the Pentecostal World Fellowship.

In 1965, the General Council of the Assemblies of God adopted a statement 'disapproving of ministers or churches participating in any of the modern ecumenical organisations ... in such a manner as to promote the Ecumenical Movement', by which was meant in particular the NCCC and the WCC. This anti-ecumenical position was reaffirmed a few years later.[7] In less antagonistic language, the Assembly of the Church of God (Cleveland) declared in 1967 that 'it saw no benefit in belonging to such an organisation (i.e. the World Council of Churches) ... due to the unique commission of the Church'.

Another sign that the barrier between the ecumenical movement and the Pentecostal movement is not entirely watertight came in 1961, when the Pentecostal Church of Chile and the Pentecostal Mission Church (also from Chile) joined the WCC, thus becoming its first Pentecostal member churches. A major earthquake had struck the southern part of the country in 1960, in the area where Chilean Pentecostalism has its roots in the mine-working communities, the poorest sector of the population. Like the Methodist Church, the cradle of the Pentecostal revival in Chile, these Pentecostal churches had a strong social commitment. They were actively engaged with other churches in working with the people, in evangelism and theological training. When they witnessed the solidarity and relief that was provided by the ecumenical fellowship to the victims of the disaster, they discovered that it was motivated by the same faith as theirs. As a natural consequence they decided to apply for membership.

The two Chilean churches were followed by the International Evangelical Church (USA, 1972), the African Church of the Holy Spirit (Kenya, 1975), the Association Church of God in Argentina (1980), the Pentecostal Mission Church of Angola (1985), the Free Pentecostal Churches of Chile (1991) and the Christian Biblical Church (Argentina, 1997). This Pentecostal presence in the fellowship of the WCC is significant because it illustrates that Pentecostal participation in institutional ecumenism is possible. However, it remains small compared with the total membership of the Council. And it is only a tiny minority when measured against the millions and millions of Pentecostals in the world.[8]

Small numbers are not always a hindrance, they can be a strength. In Latin America the large Pentecostal denominations – such as the various Assemblies of God

7. Some of these facts are taken from *A Pentecostal-Ecumenical Timeline*, an unpublished paper by Cecil M. Robeck.
8. At one point, a breakthrough seemed to have been achieved, when the 1.5 million-strong Evangelical Pentecostal Church 'Brazil for Christ', with its Charismatic leader Rev. Manoel de Mello, joined the WCC in 1969. However, this church withdrew a few years later when De Mello died.

in Brazil – are much more conservative than the more indigenous churches like
those in Chile, which are also found, among other, in Argentina, Cuba, Ecuador,
Peru and Venezuela. In the 1970s, some leaders of these communities began a
movement towards unity and cooperation, which resulted in the creation of the
Latin American Evangelical Pentecostal Commission (CEPLA in Spanish), in
1990. The Latin American Council of Churches (CLAI) and the WCC supported
this development discretely but effectively, especially through the efforts of Marta
Palma, WCC Secretary for Latin America and herself a Pentecostal from Chile,
and the General Secretary, Emilio Castro. CEPLA is an expression of ecumenical commitment that is authentically Pentecostal and Latin American. Many of
its member churches are also members of CLAI.

When, in the second half of the 20th century, the Charismatic renewal swept
through the established churches, including many of the member churches of
the WCC, yet another opportunity to bridge the gap between the movements
presented itself. Although some Pentecostals may have doubts about the Charismatic movement, because it does not necessarily emphasise speaking in tongues
as evidence of baptism in the Spirit, many see it as proof that God is shaking
the ecclesial establishment to hear the message of Pentecostalism to the
churches.

The WCC sub-unit on Renewal and Congregational Life heeded the call and initiated a discussion on 'Spirituality and the Charismatic Renewal' in 1978. It
decided to convene a consultation on the significance of the Charismatic movement for the churches. As part of the preparation, the General Secretary of the
WCC, Philip Potter, wrote a letter to the member churches inviting them to help
identify the issues which the consultation should address. The response was in
itself an indication of the degree of concern within the WCC constituency: 63
churches and organisations in various parts of the world replied and expressed
their satisfaction that the WCC was addressing a matter which they experienced
as a reality in their local situations.
The analysis of the responses brought to the fore a whole range of questions,
some pointing to the blessings of new expressions of liturgy, worship, prayer and
community life, others considering the Charismatic renewal as a culturally bound
religious phenomenon with all its ambiguities.

The consultation took place in 1980 at the Bossey Ecumenical Institute under the
theme 'A Church Renewed and United in the Spirit'. It was an event marked by
an authentic interaction of Charismatics from a wide variety of backgrounds and
those representing the WCC. The style of the meeting was a genuine mixture of
the classical mode of conducting ecumenical business – with papers and critical
theological analysis – and the narrative, celebrative and personal ways of expres-

sion of Spirit-filled believers.[9] Philip Potter himself took an active part in it and contributed a lot to the remarkable character of the consultation.

Yet the hopes and expectations raised by this event did not really materialise. The report and the recommendations it produced were accepted unanimously by the Central Committee and forwarded to the Vancouver Assembly in 1983. The sub-unit on Renewal and Congregational Life kept the Charismatic movement on its agenda. But all of this had little lasting impact on the post-assembly programme priorities of the WCC. A report on a follow-up encounter in 1984 between a group of Charismatic leaders and the sub-unit reflects the difficulties both sides had to find points of intersection where common reflection could be grafted. The intractable propensity of the WCC to re-structure itself did the rest. Renewal and Congregational Life disappeared as a distinct entity in the organisation of the Council after the Canberra Assembly in 1991.

A NEW DEPARTURE

But the Spirit blows where it wills. As the century moved to its last decade, several things happened which could be seen as unrelated but, taken together, shaped the conditions for a new departure. In August 1988, the Central Committee of the WCC decided that the Seventh Assembly in Canberra would gather under the prayer 'Come Holy Spirit – Renew the Whole Creation'. It was the first assembly theme in the history of the WCC invoking the Spirit. Whatever that implied for the Council and the ecumenical movement, it was clear from the outset that with such a theme this assembly could not afford to be unaware of Pentecostalism, its significance for the churches and the quest for unity.

As it happened, the concern was taken up in the section 'Spirit of Unity, Reconcile your People', where the issues of Faith and Order were being dealt with. One of the participants in this section was Cecil M. Robeck, the American Pentecostal theologian and scholar from Fuller Theological Seminary. Robeck, an ordained minister of the Assemblies of God, had by then been involved with Faith and Order in the USA and at WCC level for a few years, in spite of the explicit rule of his denomination against participation in the ecumenical movement (see above). Here is an illustration of the surprising respect of Pentecostals for the actions of the Spirit. Robeck had explained to the leadership of the Assemblies of God that his ecumenical ministry was in response to a call he received from the Lord. However much they disapproved, they could not exclude altogether that this was the way the Spirit wanted it. Hence Robeck was allowed to do what

---

9. See *The Church is Charismatic,* edited by Arnold Bittlinger, World Council of Churches, Geneva 1981.

he believed God was asking him to do. He reported regularly to the denomination but was not given any support. At Canberra, Robeck had a considerable share in the drafting of the paragraphs on the Pentecostal and Charismatic movements, and the formulation of the recommendations of the section regarding relationships with Pentecostals, which were eventually approved by the assembly.[10] For the first time in an official WCC document, there was an affirmation that, inasmuch as they lifted up the charisma of the Spirit described in the New Testament and embodied a rediscovery of the ministry of healing, Pentecostalism and Charismatic renewal were legitimate expressions of Christian life. The section report recognised that Pentecostals have sometimes felt excluded and accused of emotionalism, sectarianism and lack of interest for social questions by Christians of other traditions. It also noted the great diversity among Pentecostals and the different attitudes regarding the ecumenical movement, and welcomed a growing openness in the traditional churches towards the spiritual and theological perspectives of Pentecostals, especially in Latin America.

The recommendations called on the churches and the WCC to reflect anew on the gifts of the Spirit; to recognise that Pentecostal communities are part of the unfolding history of the Christian church and enrich its diversity; to encourage relations between the Pentecostal and ecumenical movements; to promote dialogue, also among Pentecostals; and to invite Pentecostals to participate in WCC activities. One recommendation was addressed particularly to Faith and Order, proposing to invite a certain number of Pentecostal theologians to join in the work of the Commission.

The Canberra assembly also marked a new stage in the capacity of the WCC to deal with relationships. As part of an internal re-organisation, an Office on Church and Ecumenical Relations was set up in the General Secretariat. It was an expression of the wish to give more attention to the nature of the Council as a fellowship of its member churches and in relation to churches outside its membership. One of the tasks given to the new Office was to build and nurture relationships with Evangelical and Pentecostal churches, groups and movements. This provided the appropriate setting to take up the assembly's recommendations on Pentecostals.

One of the first policy questions the Office had to face was whether it should seek to develop a process at the global level, like the dialogue between the Vatican and Pentecostal, or a regional approach. The latter would require more time but offered more possibilities to involve local churches and to respond better to dif-

---

10. See pages 107-108 in *Signs of the Spirit. Official Report of the Seventh Assembly*, World Council of Churches, Geneva 1991.

ferences between Pentecostals in the various regions. It was decided to opt for a process of regional consultations and to begin in Latin America, building on what had already been done in that region and on the existing network of the Latin American Evangelical Pentecostal Commission (see above).

The basic idea of the consultations was to bring together for about five days a group of some 30 persons, two-thirds of whom would be from Pentecostal churches and communities, and one-third from WCC member churches in the same country or region. The programme was conceived so as to make use as much as possible of contributions by the participants themselves – in the form of testimonies, panels, group discussions and the like – as well as one or two thematic papers prepared in advance. The themes chosen were fairly basic, such as: what is our understanding of the church; what is the mission of the church; and what is its responsibility in society?

The chief purpose was to facilitate dialogue and interaction, and to build mutual trust through a process of listening, getting to know each other and learning from one another's faith traditions. Worship, celebration and Bible study were essential components. A very important element in the early part of the programme of these consultations was to invite each person to speak about his or her personal faith journey and faith community, and to allow sufficient time for this sharing in the group. Pentecostals do this spontaneously and use such testimonies frequently as a way to get into the substance of a meeting. Christians from the traditional churches usually find this more difficult, but experience shows that they can overcome their shyness.

The meetings were left open-ended in terms of any end-product. The participants were told from the outset that they were under no obligation to produce an agreed-upon report or statement; and that it was their decision whether or not to put something in writing. It was also crucial for the integrity of the process to state clearly at the start of each meeting that there was no hidden agenda on the side of the WCC, such as wanting to gain new member churches.

The first consultation of this kind was held in 1993, in Quito, Ecuador, with a group of Evangelicals from evangelical free churches and independent churches in Latin America.[11] It was a very worthwhile experience which showed that the model could work. But its impact did not match the sparks set off by the next

---

11. Initially the Office of Church and Ecumenical Relations had the intention to carry out a broad process embracing the Evangelical, Holiness and Pentecostal traditions and the African Instituted Churches (AICs). Gradually the focus narrowed down to the latter two, and more particularly to the Pentecostals.

consultation, with Pentecostals, held in 1994, in Lima, Peru. That event was so full of energy, inspiration and enthusiasm that it immediately gave a sense of direction for the future. It was truly Pentecostal (and Latin American) in the sense that the daily timetables were not observed; some of the best discussions took place in the chapel in the midst of the celebrations; and people kept joining the meeting literally until the last day.

Instead of 30 there were over 50 participants, which knocked out the balance between WCC and Pentecostals (in their favour, of course) and made it impossible to have everybody share his or her story with the group. Stereotypes crumbled on the very first day. When a Pentecostal woman leader from Nicaragua was invited to give her testimony, she spoke as much about the unemployment and social injustice affecting the poor in her country, as about her love for Jesus and the working of the Spirit in her community. A young Pentecostal couple from Ayacucho, Peru, told in simple words how they ended up being the only pastors left in the city during the worst days of the Shining Path, and how they won the confidence of some of the guerrillas. Hearing such stories is enough to abandon the generalisation that Pentecostals are only interested in an other-worldly salvation that has nothing to do with the here and now of human history.

The consultations continued at a rhythm of one or two per year. In 1995, one was held in Leeds, England, bringing together people from the so-called 'Black-led' churches (African, Caribbean and Asian) in Great Britain – the majority of which are Pentecostal or Charismatic – and from the WCC member churches in the same country. The consultation was a joint effort with a local group of people committed to the renewal and self-affirmation of the Black-majority churches and the strengthening of their relationships.[12] Two meetings took place in 1996: one in Ogere, Nigeria, with African Instituted and mission-founded churches in West Africa; and the other in San José, Costa Rica, with Pentecostals from North America. The latter was in some respect complementary to the Lima consultation, bringing out some significant aspects of Pentecostal relationships which were less present in the encounter with the Latin Americans. It was held outside the USA, because that made it easier for the participants to accept an invitation from the WCC.

Most of the participants were scholars and all of them belonged to the large 'classical' Pentecostal denominations, namely the Assemblies of God, Church of God (Cleveland), Pentecostal Holiness Church, Church of God of Prophecy, Church

---

12. This process has since been expanded to cover other European countries (e.g. Germany, Belgium, France, Switzerland) and has resulted in the formation of the Council of Christian Communities of African Approach in Europe.

of God in Christ and Foursquare Gospel Church. These are the ones that tend to dominate the Pentecostal scene worldwide because of their mission operations and their financial power. They are generally opposed to mainstream ecumenism, if not openly hostile. Scholars from these churches may have a broader view than the leaders, but they struggle with the problem of not being heard and valued in the established academic world of theology. Most of them have been trained in theological institutions of the traditional churches and have experienced disdain for their Pentecostal identity and pressure to give it up.

Dialogue with these scholars reveals the pain felt in the Pentecostal world for the rejection by the 'mainline' churches. Besides the North Americans, there were also a few participants from Latin America at the San José meeting, some of whom had been at the Lima consultation. This added a fascinating inter-Pentecostal North-South dimension to the discussions. It showed the importance of the dialogue among Pentecostals from different ecclesial, cultural, socio-political and regional backgrounds, and the role the ecumenical movement can play in facilitating opportunities where this can happen.

In 1997, a pan-African consultation with African Instituted Churches was held in Limuru, Kenya, in cooperation with the Nairobi-based Organisation of African Instituted Churches. Later that year a modest but notable step forward was made in the relationships with Pentecostals. A group of them were invited to a meeting with the WCC at the Bossey Ecumenical Institute. Several of the Pentecostal participants had been at one or other of the previous consultations; others came from regions where no meetings had as yet been organised and were therefore new to the process.[13]

Part of the background for this event was the need to assess Pentecostal relationships in preparation for the upcoming Eighth Assembly of the WCC. The WCC was represented by the General Secretary, Konrad Raiser; the Director of Faith and Order, Alan Falconer; and other senior staff. In addition to the dialogue's usual pattern, this meeting also addressed some specific and potentially controversial issues, such as common witness and proselytism, and church unity.

Towards the end of their time together, the two parties met separately to review the exercise and consider possible suggestions for the future. When they shared their findings, it turned out that both were proposing that an official WCC-Pentecostal dialogue be initiated and a group be formed for this purpose. It may have been a mere meeting of minds, but there was also a sense that the Spirit was at

---

13. Plans to hold regional consultations in Africa, Asia and Europe had been postponed for reasons of lack of time and human and financial resources.

work that day in two adjacent rooms, bringing to fruition what had been a long haul!

To complete the picture of these years, it would be necessary to expand on the wealth of relationships and mutual trust which gradually developed as a result of the consultations that were held. The personal encounter with the other is by far the best means to open hearts and minds and change the attitudes of people and institutions which are separated by oceans of misgivings, ignorance and suspicion. Each meeting required the tedious job of searching for names and addresses (often with the help of a third person), establishing contacts, explaining the purpose time and again, sending reminders, clarifying misunderstandings, persuading persons with fully booked agendas whose presence could make a difference, and the like. Each meeting was a venture into the unknown and mistakes were unavoidable. But each meeting paid off and contributed to enlarging the circle. One of the outcomes of these efforts was the large number of Pentecostals and representatives of African Instituted churches who attended the Eighth Assembly in Harare, in 1998, as delegated observers (for the first time), observers or visitors.

The Assembly gave its official approval to the proposal to set up a 'joint working group of the WCC and Pentecostals'.[14] The name was later changed to 'Joint Consultative Group' in order to avoid confusion with the Joint Working Group of the WCC and the Roman Catholic Church. Two parent bodies mandate the latter, which is not the case of the group with Pentecostals. Telling the story of the Joint Consultative Group, which has met annually from 2000 to 2005, will have to wait until it has fulfilled its term and presented its report to the Ninth Assembly of the WCC, in February 2006, in Porto Alegre, Brazil. One thing is sure already: the group will unanimously recommend that the 'Pentecostals-Ecumenicals Dialogue' be continued.

---

14. See pages 167-168 in *Together on the Way. Official Report of the Eighth Assembly*, World Council of Churches, Geneva 1999.

7. What Can the Mainline learn from Pentecostals about Pentecost?[1]

Cheryl Bridges Johns

Pentecostalism is a strange and sometimes frightening form of Christianity. In an age in which Protestant worship is characterized by order and reasoned discourse, Pentecostal worship seems to promote chaos. Persons seized by the Spirit may roll on the floor, cry uncontrollably, run in the aisles, speak in tongues, and fall into extended trances. Some are even known to handle snakes. Moreover, preaching in such a context seems to be all style and little substance.

Because of its strangeness and because Pentecostalism has been routinely dismissed as an escapist religion for the socially disenfranchised, it has been easy for those in the mainline tradition to ignore the movement. However, it is getting more and more difficult to do so. The Charismatic renewal has brought much of the life and energy of Pentecostalism into the traditional churches. In addition, the sheer numerical scope of the movement, which is estimated at over 400 million, makes it difficult to ignore.

It is now somewhat acceptable to study Pentecostalism in order to glean those aspects which may enrich all of Christian worship. More and more, there are 'Pentecostal-type' services found in mainline and Roman Catholic circles. While I don't want to negate the integral impact of praise choruses, healing services, testimony meetings and spontaneous prayers, I believe that we all are missing the larger questions of the gifts and calling of Pentecostalism for the whole body of Christ.

It is my contention that the primary mission of Pentecostalism is to renew the meaning of Pentecost for the whole church. While it is not uncommon today to find references to Pentecost as a means of renewal of human community, redressing the curses of the present post-modern state of Babel,[2] Pentecost remains a

---

1. This article was published earlier in *Journal for Preachers* XXI/4 (Pentecost 1998).
2. In particular, see Anthony Thiselton, *Interpreting God and the Postmodern Self* (Grand Rapids: Eerdmans, 1995); J. Richard Middleton and Brian and J. Walsh, *Truth is Stranger Than It Used to Be* (Downers Grove: InterVarsityPress, 1995).

largely unexplored theological construct. For most Protestants, Pentecost is viewed as a static historical event with little ongoing meaning and signification other than its place within the liturgical year.

Paul Vallarie, in his creative and thought-provoking analysis of Pentecost, attributes this lack of interest to the association of 'Pentecostal themes' with fundamentalism, pietism and anti-intellectualism. He points out that modern-day Pentecostalism is part of the church but not the whole, and it should not be put forward as the measure of Pentecostal religion. Vallarie defines Pentecostal religion as one which takes its stand not on the letter of the law but in the presence of the Spirit and in freedom. He calls for the theological inquiry regarding the meaning of Pentecost for the whole *oikonomia*.[3]

I would concur with Vallarie's assessment and with his view that modern-day Pentecostalism is not the full measure of Pentecost for the church today. Pentecost belongs to the whole church and not to any particular group. All Christian churches are Pentecostal churches. However, I would also want to point out that Pentecostalism, in its attempt to redress the meaning of Pentecost, offers clues as to its significance for today. There are 'signs of Pentecost' inherent within the Pentecostal movement which have dramatic implications for the church's ministry as we enter a new millennium. In this brief article, I would like to focus on four of these signs: Pentecost as an ongoing festival; Pentecost as the epistemological key; Pentecost as a festival of deconstruction and reconstruction; and Pentecost as a marginal festival.

PENTECOST AS AN ONGOING FESTIVAL

The Day of Pentecost as recorded in Acts 2, was celebrated as part of the Feast of Weeks. Originally a spring-time harvest festival, in later Jewish tradition it had come to commemorate the giving of the Law at Sinai. The theophany of God in the wilderness provided a reality and a way ahead for a people who were in a liminal state of 'in-betweenness'.

The coming of the Spirit in Jerusalem occurred among post-resurrection believers who were also in a liminal state of 'in-betweenness'. Faced with the collapse of their meta-narrative and the absence of Christ, the disciples were waiting for a way ahead. The storm of God's presence which arrived with wind and fire, not only filled the vacuum left by the absence of Christ, but reordered the known world of the disciples, providing a renewed sense of identity and mission. In addi-

---

3. Paul Vallarie, *Holy War and Pentecostal Peace* (New York: Seabury Press, 1983), pp. 4, 5.

tion, the Acts events enlarged the boundaries of the household of faith to include 'all flesh'. The Spirit of Life, the Creator Spirit, was being sent to renew the whole created order into the economy of God through Christ.

This power unleashed upon the world on the Day of Pentecost continues to burn as the ongoing life-giving fuel for the church. Pentecost is therefore an ongoing festival of fear, joy, and power.

To celebrate Pentecost is not to recall an event which is locked in time and space. Rather, it is to participate in a continuing festival which is ever more mysterious, frightening, and wonderful than we can dare imagine. Pentecost Festival brings to us the power and guidance of the Holy Spirit, who is being sent to lead us into all truth. Pentecost Festival is thus our way ahead into an unknown future. It gives us direction and a sense of mission and purpose.

Pentecost Festival is ever enlarging to include 'all flesh'. It celebrates the fulfilment of ancient prophecies that all people, from the least to the greatest, can know God. To participate in Pentecost is to celebrate the longing and desires of God to redeem the whole created order.

To celebrate Pentecost is to celebrate and participate in the ecstasy of God toward us. It is a festival in which the work of Christ, making a way to God for us, is brought into fulfilment. Pentecost is thus a great celebration of the plan of redemption. It actualizes the longing and desires of God for the whole economy.

Pentecost Festival celebrates the power of the Holy Spirit to bring us into union and communion with God. Indeed, we are literally swept into the ecstatic embrace of the Trinity. The shining countenance of God is turned toward us and we are invited into the one Divine life. Pentecost is a celebration that we are not left orphaned (John 14.18), having to make our way alone.

Therefore, to celebrate Pentecost is more than acknowledging that at a certain point in time the Holy Spirit was sent. It is to acknowledge that the Holy Spirit is continually being poured out upon humanity, ever renewing the face of the church. This ongoing festival continually calls us to participate in the work of the Holy Spirit.

Pentecost offers to the church a continual transformation of itself. It is ever pushing forward into the realm of the unknown and ever surprising with its power. It infuses the church with the mission of Christ and empowers it to accomplish what seems to be the impossible. The festival of Pentecost offers continual amazement as we see with our own eyes the work of the Holy Spirit. We can indeed see the goodness of the Lord in the land of the living.

Pentecost As The Epistemological Key

A mainline friend once asked me why we Pentecostals emphasized the Feast of Pentecost. He pointed out that Pentecost is only one event of salvation history which the church celebrates. 'Does not the emphasis upon Pentecost downplay the other feasts: the Birth, Death, Resurrection of Christ?' he asked. His question forced me to examine my tradition's apparent overemphasis on this Christian festival.

The Feast of Pentecost, rather than downplaying or overshadowing the importance of the other feasts, brings alive their meaning. It is through the power of Pentecost that we have knowledge of the depths and mysteries of salvation history. Pentecost is thus a portal or a doorway into a realm of knowing which may be characterized as face-to-face knowing.

In his Last Words (John 14-17), Jesus promises to send the Holy Spirit who would become a 'second Christ', teaching and leading the disciples into all truth.[4] This form of knowing makes alive the presence of Christ. Like the disciples on the road to Emmaus, our eyes are opened and we understand. We revisit salvation history. The Spirit, like a time machine, takes us back to Sinai, Bethlehem and to Calvary.

The meaning of scripture is made known by the power of Pentecost. Because of the ongoing ministry of the Holy Spirit, the text of scripture, as written word, is alive and powerful. Spirit and word are fused together into a *gestalt* which reveals the mysteries of God. It is more than a revelation of meaning; it is a revelation of God, whose presence is actualized by the Holy Spirit.

What is also revealed are the mysteries found in the depths of being human. Pentecost causes the Word of God to cut deep into the hidden recesses of the heart, convicting of sin and righteousness. This unveiling of reality, which supersedes any form of human critical reflection, makes known those things which are masked, repressed, and denied. The form of criticism emerging from Pentecost causes the so-called Enlightenment criticism to pale in comparison!

---

4. Raymond Brown, 'The Paraclete in the Fourth Gospel'. In: *New Testament Studies* 13 (1967) pp. 12-124.

PENTECOST AS FESTIVAL OF DECONSTRUCTION AND RECONSTRUCTION

Inherent within Pentecostalism is the sign that Pentecost is a powerful *gestalt* of deconstruction and reconstruction with the ability to tear apart and dismantle as well as to unite and create order.

The deconstructive side of Pentecost is that which is most disturbing to the modem mind. It makes it difficult to 'mainline'. There are few theological constructs available to interpret its meaning. Even liberation theology with its voice for the poor and its challenges to the power interests of modem theology, has left intact the human subject with its power to name the world.

But Pentecost refuses to leave the human subject intact. The festival of Pentecost exposes the fallacy of the human subject being grounded in its own self-presence. It mocks the pretentious claims that humans make their own history. Instead, it offers a presence which interrupts the known world with both promise and judgment (recall Peter's sermon on the Day of Pentecost and his references to Joel 2.28).

In many ways, Pentecost is an apocalypse of the self which calls for a relinquishing of the desire for control and totality. To participate in Pentecost is to desire God above all else. It is to surrender those things which we hold most dear. It is to surrender those myths which we believe to be true about ourselves: that we are able to live independently; that we are in need of nothing outside of ourselves. It is to enter into a frightening realm of the possibility of death of all we hold dear and understand.

In Pentecost, human subjects become 'eschatological selves', whose place is transported into the eternal space of God's presence. Here human existence is grounded into the existence of God. We become one with God and God becomes one with us. In this sacred space we may experience tears and groaning, having been overwhelmed by the longing and the flow of the pathos of God. The Spirit, flowing through the self, groans, longing for the day of restoration of the whole cosmos. At other times, we may laugh hysterically, seemingly overcome by a continual flow of joy.

The reconstructive work of the Holy Spirit resurrects from deconstruction into a newly configured sense of identity. Grounded in Trinitarian fellowship, persons are no longer passive victims of destructive and manipulative forces. As reconstituted agents, they are thrust upon mission. What is primary in this sense of mission is not praxis (critical reflection and action) but rather participation, 'the

taste of the good that is also the goal'.[5] Having tasted of the goodness of God
and having been touched by the Divine longing flowing from the heart of God,
persons are compelled into mission. There is a sense of participating in the Spirit's
mission and agenda.

Often ecumenical discussions and documents regarding proselytism do not take
into account the compulsion felt by many Pentecostals to share the good news
of Pentecost with others. To experience the overwhelming, sheer excess of God's
Spirit, many times results in the transgressing of boundaries. Certainly there are
those occasions when Pentecostals have been guilty of a lack of regard for the
real presence of Christ in other traditions. However, what is more often the case
is a genuine enthusiasm and desire that all taste of the freedom and joy of the
Holy Spirit.

By the power of the Holy Spirit, Jesus is today walking among the poor, offering healing and hope. The celebration of Pentecost is a celebration of this presence of Christ. It is the celebration of a power which lifts the lowly and tears
down the proud. What is there to lose in the apocalypse of Pentecost? Power,
prestige, status, dignity, self-control, all these have already been taken away by
oppressive, demonic powers. What is gained is a renewed and transformed vision
of the power to overcome and a newfound sense of identity and dignity.

PENTECOST AS A MARGINAL FESTIVAL

What disturbs me the most about attempts to mainline Pentecost, as evidenced
in much of the Charismatic movement and in many middle-class Pentecostal
churches, is the tendency to tame or domesticate the power of the Holy Spirit.
This domesticated form of Pentecostalism seeks to view Pentecost spirituality as
providing a fuller and richer Christian life, without all of the danger and scan-
dal associated with such an experience. It attempts to behave itself, so that it can
fit into existing liturgical and ecclesial structures.

What is lost in mainlined Pentecostalism is the understanding that Pentecost is
a festival which by its very nature defies being co-opted by human agendas.
Indeed, Pentecost seems to mock all attempts to contain its power. For that reason, it is most clearly experienced in the margins. Pentecost is a marginal festival which marginalizes all who dare participate.

The modern church seems obsessed with a desire to be central, to have voice and
influence in the centers of power. Yet it is being more marginalized in the newly

---

5. Vallarie, p. 25.

emerging culture of pluralism. Pentecost calls us to relinquish this desire for centrality. It calls us to its own core, its own center of power and authority. Around this core, people from every nation are united in a new form of human community.

The community of Pentecost is characterized by the freedom of the Holy Spirit to direct and to determine its character. Within this community the gifts of the Spirit are given to members without regard to 'official categories'. Indeed, the Spirit seems to delight in creating what appears to be a 'feast of fools'. The values and positions of the dominant culture seem to be turned upside down by Pentecost. An illiterate peasant may be given great knowledge and discernment, and the discourse of the educated may be reduced to babbling tongues.

In order to find Pentecost Festival today, we must journey into the wondrous and wild realm of the margins. There we may encounter an 'upper room', where the dispossessed are tarrying and waiting for a way ahead. If we push into that which disturbs and frightens us about 'those people', we may find the liberating power of Pentecost awaiting us in their arms.

8. Guidelines for a Challenging Dialogue with Pentecostals: Lessons from the Netherlands

Paul van der Laan

When I finished my dissertation[1] in 1988 on Pentecostalism in ecumenical perspective, one could hardly have foreseen how relevant this topic would become in the following decades. It was the focus of the fall 1995 issue of the SPS (Society for Pentecostal Studies) periodical *Pneuma*.[2] In 2002, the SPS devoted its conference theme to the same topic[3] and stated that it had a promising future, as more and more scholars were entering into this process. Cecil M. Robeck concluded:

> Pentecostal interest and participation in ecumenism are still in their infancy. Those who enter the field at this time will help to define the field for the future of Pentecostal participation. A variety of churches and organizations exist, which are open to Pentecostal participation. The building of bridges between denominations is a rewarding challenge that can bear good fruit .[4]

The international dialogue with the Roman Catholic Church is still continuing and is now in its sixth quinquennium. The international dialogue between representatives of the World Alliance of Reformed Churches and some classical Pentecostal churches and leaders is in its second quinquennium.[5]

---

1. Paul van der Laan, 'The Question of Spiritual Unity. The Dutch Pentecostal Movement in Ecumenical Perspective', PhD dissertation, University of Birmingham, 1988.
2. *Pneuma, The Journal of the Society for Pentecostal Studies*, 17/2, Fall 1995, pp. 145-228.
3. Society for Pentecostal Studies, *Pentecostalism and the World Church: Ecumenical Opportunities and Challenges*, 31st Annual Meeting, Lakeland, Florida, March 14-16, 2002. The SPS set up the Ecumenical Interest Group in 2000.
4. Cecil M. Robeck Jr., *Pentecostals and Christian Unity: Facing the Challenge*, p. 19. Presentation at the 31st Annual Meeting of the SPS in Lakeland, Florida on March 15, 2002. The paper is not included in the documentation of the meeting, but is available at the SPS homepage: *www.sps-usa.org*.
5. *Word and Spirit, Church and Word.* The Final Report of the International Dialogue between Representatives of the World Alliance of Reformed Churches and Some Classical Pentecostal Churches and Leaders 1996-2000. In: *Pneuma, The Journal of the Society for Pentecostal Churches*, 23/1 (Spring 2001) pp. 9-37.

The ecumenical dialogue that flourished in the Netherlands after 1988, was beyond my wildest dreams. Various national dialogues began, of which two are still ongoing. The dialogue with the Reformed Churches in the Netherlands (*Gereformeerde Kerken in Nederland*, GKN) lasted for three years (1992-1995). The dialogue with a number of interdenominational missionary organisations began in 1998. The most recent dialogue with the Roman Catholic Church started in 1999.

The author was privileged to participate in all of these dialogues as a Pentecostal delegate. In this article, I would like to follow up on my dissertation of 1988 by trying to summarize what additional lessons can be learned from these recent interactions and producing some guidelines for a challenging dialogue with Pentecostals, using the Netherlands as a role model.

Many other significant developments that have taken place during this period are not included in this study, such as the growth of the indigenous migrant churches; the Alpha courses; the merger of the two largest Pentecostal denominations in the country to form the Assemblies of God in the Netherlands (*Verenigde Pinkster- en Evangelie Gemeenten*, VPE; literally the United Pentecostal and Evangelical Churches) in 2002; the integration of the Azusa Theological College (including the establishment of an academic chair in Pentecostalism) at the Free University of Amsterdam; and the merger of the Netherlands Reformed Church (*Nederlands Hervormde Kerk*, NHK), the GKN and the Dutch Lutheran church to form the Protestant Church in the Netherlands (*Protestantse Kerk in Nederland*, PKN) in 2004. While these events are not somehow less significant, the author has chosen to limit his investigation for this article to those events where an ecumenical exchange has taken place.

DIALOGUE WITH THE REFORMED CHURCHES IN THE NETHERLANDS

In 1976, the synod of the GKN decided to appoint some delegates for the study of the Charismatic movement, in particular with reference to the issues of church offices and baptism.[6] This resulted in a positive evaluation of the Charismatic movement, leading to the decision to give this committee a more permanent mandate to continue the dialogue with the Charismatic Movement in the Nether-

---

6. Acta van de Generale Synode [Proceedings of the General Synod] van Maastricht 1975-1976 van de Gereformeerde Kerken in Nederland (Kampen: Kok); meeting of October 7, 1976, acta art. 332, p. 216.

lands, who had organized themselves as the so-called CWN (*Charismatische Werkgemeenschap Nederland*).[7]

In 1992, I challenged this committee to open a dialogue with the Brotherhood of Pentecostal Churches (*Broederschap van Pinkstergemeenten*, hereafter referred to as the Brotherhood), which at that time had recently appointed a committee for this purpose. To my delight, they reacted positively to this suggestion.[8] Among those taking part in this dialogue were a representative of the GKN's ecumenism committee and a representative of the CWN. The committee met seven times with various representatives of the Brotherhood over a period of more than two years.[9] All meetings were held in the GKN's national secretariat in Leusden and chaired by Riemer Roukema of the GKN committee. In her report to the GKN synod, the committee concluded that 'they had experienced these conversations as open and fruitful'.[10] In mutual agreement the following topics were discussed:

1. The perception church members have of the Pentecostal movement
2. The perception Pentecostals have of the church
3. Transfer of members from the mainline churches to Pentecostal denominations and vice versa
4. Prophecy
5. Ethics and pastoral care

Let me summarize the main conclusions of these discussions, which may serve to illustrate how an open dialogue can be of mutual benefit.

---

7. In 1984, the delegates issued a booklet to 'help in the discussions about and with the Charismatic movement'. 'Deputaten voor Contact met de Charismatische Werkgemeenschap Nederland, Vurig van Geest – Een handreiking voor gesprekken over en met de charismatische beweging'. In the *Toerusting* series (Driebergen: Centrale voor vormingswerk, 1984).
8. Bijlagen bij de Acta van de Generale Synode [Appendices to the Proceedings of the General Synod] van Aalten 1993 van de Gereformeerde Kerken in Nederland (Kampen: Kok, 1995), p. 155.
9. Usually about five to six Pentecostals took part. Regular attendees were Paul Pouwelse (chaplain), Ap van Polen (retired pastor), Klaas van Balen (pastor), Paul van der Laan and Huib Zegwaart (general secretary of the Brotherhood). Committee members of the GKN who participated were E.A. de Boer, T. de Jong, C. van der Kooi, R.A. van Kooij, R. Roukema (chair) and B.C. van Wieren. The GKN ecumenism committee was represented by the P. Schravendeel or L.J. Koffeman. The CWN was represented by the W.W. Verhoef.
10. Bijlagen bij de Acta van de Generale Synode van Haren 1995 van de Gereformeerde Kerken in Nederland (Kampen: Kok, 1997), p. 499.

The perception church members have of the Pentecostal movement[11]

- The Pentecostal movement holds a great attraction for people who are looking for fulfillment in their life.
- Pentecostals sing enthusiastically and use a variety of musical instruments.
- There is earnest prayer and experiential preaching.
- They pray with the sick and have a practical involvement of their faith.
- Pentecostals tend to look upon themselves as superior compared to ordinary church members.
- In many Pentecostal churches, there is rivalry between the pastor, elders and members.
- On ethical issues, the Bible is used too quickly and too univocal.
- The preaching is quite elementary.
- Infant baptism is not accepted and believers who want to join a Pentecostal church need to be re-baptized.

The perception Pentecostals have of the church[12]

The Pentecostals seem to have a more negative perception of the church:

- There is little spiritual life, especially with regard to prayer and the relation with God.
- There is insufficient openness for the work of the Holy Spirit.
- There is a great lack of sanctification.
- The theological education is too much geared to the intellectual.
- Biblical exegesis and hermeneutics are too liberal.
- The liturgy is too static, old-fashioned and impersonal.
- There is too little personal contact among the members.
- The churches are too much engaged in politics and social help, instead of emphasizing the vertical relation with God and the evangelization of the world.
- The distance between God and humans is too big in the church.

Committee members of the GKN were of the opinion that a number of these issues were outdated and no longer relevant.

---

11. Bijlagen bij de Acta van de Generale Synode van Haren 1995 van de Gereformeerde Kerken in Nederland (Kampen: Kok, 1997), pp. 499-500.
12. Ibid, pp. 500-502.

Transfer of members[13]

Reasons why members of the GKN transferred to a Pentecostal church:[14]

- Enthusiastic Christianity
- The songs and music in the Pentecostal church
- Adult baptism by immersion
- Appealing sermons and call to conversion
- Warm social involvement with one another
- The security of life that is offered
- Active church programmes for children
- Former personal experiences with the Holy Spirit, which are acknowledged by the Pentecostals

Reasons why Pentecostals join the GKN:

- More liberty and tolerance
- More openness for different opinions
- Room for homosexuals and acceptance of their lifestyle
- More profound preaching and Biblical exposition
- A broader view of the church and of church tradition

Prophecy[15]

The Pentecostals indicated that they were suspicious when a prophet re-affirms himself (or herself) in his (or her) position. The community of believers should test the prophets, and a prophet who does not want his or her prophecies to be tested, cannot be trusted. Prophecies have a tendency to confirm the status quo and lose their critical effect. The routine of having prophecies sometimes results in them not being taken too seriously.

The GKN delegates added that Pentecostals only seem to be open for a specific type of prophecy. According to them, the repeated urging by a church member or of a particular passage in a sermon may also be prophetic. The pacifists who demon-

---

13. Ibid, p. 502.
14. In the period 1954-1985, a total of 5,245 members of the GKN transferred to a Pentecostal church. In that same period, 196 Pentecostals transferred to the GKN. Source: *Jaarboek van de Gereformeerde Kerken* 1956-1987 (Goes: Oosterbaan & Le Cointre); chapter 'Statistiek – section Grensverkeer'. Also Paul van der Laan, *The Question of Spiritual Unity*, p. 476.
15. Bijlagen bij de Acta van de Generale Synode van Haren 1995 van de Gereformeerde Kerken in Nederland (Kampen: Kok, 1997), p. 503.

strated for nuclear disarmament also experienced the prophetic nature of their manifestations. Pentecostals are generally reluctant to make prophetic utterances on political issues, but there is increasingly an awareness of social and political abuses.

Ethics and pastoral care[16]

Pentecostals have a strong sense of community and provide shelter for many who have social or psychological problems. As a result of their holiness heritage, Pentecostals have ethical reservations on issues such as sex before marriage and divorce. There is a tendency to spiritualize or demonize a social or psychological problem. It was acknowledged that the mainline churches usually provide more balanced and professional care in these cases.

At the end of the dialogue, the GKN committee concluded that this had been 'a genuine dialogue. From both sides there was a readiness to critically observe one's own denominational tradition and to hold the other "party" accountable for the questions and criticism that were raised'.[17] They recommended to continue this dialogue, but unfortunately this never happened. I must add that the Pentecostals also did not initiate a continuation. From my personal observations, I would like to add the following comments:

- The dialogue was the most intensive and genuine so far. There was indeed a surprising openness, and the Pentecostals were treated as equal partners.
- All meetings were held in the GKN national secretariat and chaired by their committee, which created a feeling of ownership and dominance by the GKN.
- I personally challenged the GKN members to allow time for mutual worship so as to 'get a taste of our spiritual life'. Although some of the Reformed delegates were open to this, it never materialized. The dialogue therefore remained merely an intellectual exchange.
- Essential topics like pneumatology, baptism, divine healing, signs and miracles, evangelism and missions, were not addressed. The Pentecostals could also have reflected on the various documents produced by the GKN committee.[18] There seems still to be plenty to talk about.

---

16. Ibid, pp. 503-504. For this meeting, Connie Karsten, professor at the Azusa Theological College (Brotherhood) was invited to give an introduction.
17. *Ibid*, p. 504.
18. *Bulletin voor Charismatische Theologie* , 4/7 (Easter 1981) pp. 2-16; and 6/11 (Spring 1983) pp. 3-19; and 9/18 (Autumn 1986) pp. 3-14. 'Profetieën, ingevingen en visioenen. Omgaan met bijzondere ervaringen,' Bijlagen bij de Acta van de Generale Synode van Haren 1995 van de Gereformeerde Kerken in Nederland (Kampen: Kok, 1997), p. 474-498.

The following two dialogues which I introduce here are still ongoing. For this reason, I will merely focus on their initial history and some of their more remarkable characteristics.

MISSIOLOGICAL INTERACTION AND VISION

In 1996, the delegates of the Netherlands Missionary Council (*Nederlandse Zendingsraad*, NZR)[19] were astonished that there were no representatives of the (black) Pentecostal churches at the Conference on World Mission and Evangelism in Salvador, Brazil. When they questioned the conference leadership about this, they were challenged by the latter and the staff of the World Council of Churches in Geneva, to start a dialogue with the national Pentecostal and Charismatic organizations. The NZR's general secretary, Wout van Laar, had already taken up a personal interest in the Pentecostal movement during the years he lived and worked in Chile.

Together with the Evangelical Missionary Alliance (*Evangelische Zendingsalliantie*, EZA)[20] and the Netherlands Mission Council (*Nederlandse Missieraad*, NMR),[21] the NZR organized a 'day of meeting and consultation' on May 12, 1998. The goal of this meeting was 'to get to know and recognize Christians of the Ecumenical, Charismatic and Pentecostal traditions, in the hope that in this meeting and celebration a new vision may grow for cooperation and unity in the unified mission of God (*Missio Dei*)'.[22] More than 50 representatives of these various traditions took part, including members of the migrant churches. The main speaker was Cheryl Bridges John,[23] who was introduced as an 'American Pentecostal theologian'. The day concluded with worship and prayer. This resulted in the formation of the Missionary Quarterly Council (*Missionair kwartaalberaad*). During its first session in January 1999, Prof. Walter Hollenweger introduced a number of suggestions for an effective dialogue. The group agreed to pursue the following aims:[24]

---

19. See Wout van Laar, *Introduction* of this book.
20. About 70 evangelical missionary organizations in the Netherlands cooperate in the EZA. For a complete list of their participants and more information, consult their Dutch website at *www.eza.nl*.
21. The NMR coordinates the activities in the Roman Catholic Church in the Netherlands with regard to mission, development aid and dialogue. For more information, consult their Dutch website at *www.missieraad.nl*.
22. Wout van Laar, *Missionair Kwartaalberaad – Een terugblik*, (Amsterdam: Nederlandse Zendingsraad, 2001), 123/01, p. 1.
23. The core of her lecture is published in her article 'Cheryl Bridges Johns, What Can the Mainline Learn from Pentecostals about Pentecost', p. 93-99 of this publication.
24. Wout van Laar, *Missionair Kwartaalberaad – Een Terugblik*, p. 2.

- The Missionary Quarterly Council aims to create a forum where 15-20 participants meet informally in a hospitable environment.
- The meetings must include moments of celebration and prayer. There needs to be a fruitful balance between heart and mind, worship and discussion.
- The council wants to initiate a learning process in which we get to know one another in such a way that it will remove our prejudices and lead to possible ways of cooperation in a missiological perspective.
- The meetings cannot be merely investigative and non-committal. It is our goal to develop a framework for a combined missiological strategy for the 21st century.

During the following meetings,[25] a wide range of topics were discussed. In chronological order, they were: the strength and weakness of Pentecostal mission; eschatology as motive for mission; intercultural theology and narrative exegesis; our testimony and to be a witness; African Pentecostalism; non-Western Pentecostalism in the Netherlands, and christology. One of the most significant features of this dialogue was the time of worship and prayer, usually at the beginning of each session. In his report on the first three years of these meetings, Van Laar described this as follows:

> What cannot be reported are the experiences during the moments of celebration and fellowship, which are the heart of the Missionary Quarterly Council. These recurring moments, when we light the candle and are silent together in the face of God and call out his name. When we worship Him, it brings the participants closer to one another and these moments are invaluable.[26]

Another important element is the inclusion of the migrant churches, which form the fastest growing section of the Pentecostal family in the Netherlands[27] and bring home the Great Commission in the real sense of the word. During the council's meeting on June 4, 2003, Cees van der Kooi said that it is wishful thinking to achieve unified mission engagement in the Netherlands, so long as the 'white

---

25. Meetings were held on January 1, 1999; September 2, 1999; November 4, 1999; February 3, 2000; May 18, 2000; September 14, 2000; January 1, 2001 (hosted by the African Pentecostal Council of Churches); May 17, 2001; January 21, 2002; February 27-29, 2003 (Symposium in conjunction with the inauguration of the Pentecostal Academic Chair and the opening of the Hollenweger Center at the Free University of Amsterdam) and June 4, 2003.

26. Wout van Laar, *Missionair Kwartaalberaad – Een terugblik*, p. 9.

27. A.P. van der Broek, *Migrant Churches*, lecture at the symposium on non-Western Pentecostalism in the Netherlands, Free University of Amsterdam, February 27-28, 2003.

churches' are not clear about the position of Jesus Christ and sustain their vague pneumatology.[28]

These meetings still seem to be in the exploratory phase. It will be interesting to see whether a combined missiological strategy can be formulated. The mutual recognition, dialogue combined with worship, and the balanced participation may prove to be the right ingredients to reach this challenging goal.

THE HOLY CONFUSION OF ROMAN CATHOLIC CHARISMATICS

In 1997, Peter Hocken[29] visited the Catholic Charismatic Renewal in the Netherlands. His lecture stimulated their National Pastoral Core Group (*Landelijk Pastorale Kerngroep*) to invite the Brotherhood to appoint a delegate to attend their annual conferences. In their letter of July 10, 1998 they wrote:

> We are impressed by the outpouring of the Spirit over so may Christians, who plant so many new churches, apart from the historical churches. It is not important whether we do or do not like this because of our own denominational perception; whether we agree with it or not; or whether all is perfect or not. It is important [to recognize] that the Holy Spirit is at work. That is why we are directly involved in this by the same Spirit. In essence, there is a unity because we are baptized in the same Spirit. That is why we believe that the Lord is urging us to be in closer personal relationship with you.[30]

The Brotherhood responded positively and appointed me as their delegate to represent them at their annual conference. This contact and the desire to discuss

---

28. See Cornelis van der Kooi, 'The Challenge of Migrant Churches', p. 115-124 of this book; also W. van Laar, 'Vage Geest-theologie barrière voor dialoog', *Wereld en zending*, 2003/3, p. 112-113.
29. Peter Hocken served as an officer of the Society for Pentecostal Studies, second vice-president, first vice-president, president (1983-1986) and executive secretary (1988-1997). In March 2001, he was appointed as a chaplain to His Holiness the Pope, at the request of his bishop, Leo of Northampton, UK. He presently lives in Vienna, Austria. He has written several books on the Charismatic movement and ecumenism: *Streams of Renewal* (Paternoster, 1986), *One Lord One Spirit One Body* (Paternoster, 1987), The *Glory and the Shame* (Eagle, 1994), *The Strategy of the Spirit?* (Eagle, 1996), *Blazing the Trail* (Alive, 2001), *The Spirit of Unity: How Renewal is Breaking Down Barriers between Evangelicals and Roman Catholics* (Grove, 2001).
30. National Pastoral Core Group of the Catholic Charismatic Renewal in the Netherlands [Landelijk Pastorale Kerngroep, Katholieke Charismatische Vernieuwing in Nederland], letter to the Brotherhood of Pentecostal Churches in the Netherlands, July 10, 1998, in Kees Slijkerman, *Als wij niet willen roept God anderen.*

the report of the fourth phase (1990-1997) of the international dialogue between the Roman Catholic Church and some classical Pentecostal churches and leaders on 'Evangelization, Proselytism and Common Witness',[31] resulted in the decision to start a national dialogue between representatives of the Catholic Charismatic Renewal and the Brotherhood. We decided to meet every four months with about 10 representatives from each denomination. The delegates should include clergy and laity, and represent various age groups. The two denominations were to alternate in hosting the meetings.

A core group of two representatives from each denomination prepared these meetings and drew up the agenda. Each meeting was to start with a time of charismatic worship, personal testimony, prayer and prophecy. I insisted on this, because I knew that many Pentecostals were prejudiced towards the Charismatic Catholics. They could not figure out how somebody could be baptized in the Spirit and still pray to Mary or, even more horrifying, smoke a pipe. I knew from experience that the best way to overcome this prejudice was to have Charismatic interaction with them. The holy confusion would result in the undeniable acknowledgment that it is the same Spirit and the same gifts so familiar to us as Pentecostals.

After the worship, a delegate of each denomination would introduce the day's topic, which we then discussed in small groups and/or in plenary. This set-up has worked remarkably well. The dialogue is still ongoing and nine meetings have to date taken place:[32]

1. November 11, 1999 – 'Our mutual perception of one another'
2. March 2, 2000 – 'The ministry of healing'
3. June 14, 2000 – 'The pastoral contact with our sick neighbour'
4. November 15-16, 2000[33] – 'God's word in humn words'
5. June 18, 2001 – 'Consultation on publication of a report of the dialogue about healing'
6. November 29, 2001 – 'The Church of Jesus Christ and its necessary structures'

---

31. Published in *Information Service* 97 (1998/ I-II) of the Pontifical Council for Promoting Christian Unity, Vatican City.
32. Kees Slijkerman, *Chronologisch overzicht van de eerste fase van dialoog in Nederland, 1999-2002*, November 14, 2002; and press release, *Oecumenische dialoog naar een nieuw model – Achtste Dialoogdag van katholieken en pinkstergelovigen*. Most of the lectures presented at these meetings and additional information about this dialogue are published in Kees Slijkerman, *Inhoudsopgave Nederlandse dialoog rkk-pinksteren*.
33. This two-day meeting took place in the Achelse Kluis monastery. Delegates participated in the prayer sessions with the monks.

7. April 12, 2002 – 'Evangelization, proselytism and common witness'
8. November 27, 2002 – 'A new model for ecumenical dialogue – Consultation with Fr. Peter Hocken'
9. November 18, 2003 – 'The Pentecostal perception of the Lord's Supper and union of Christ in the eucharist'

The meetings were also attended by a delegate of the Catholic Society for Ecumenism (*Katholieke Vereniging voor Oecumene*). In 2002, the Brotherhood merged with the Full Gospel Churches Netherlands (*Volle Evangelie Gemeenten Nederland*), the second largest Pentecostal denomination in the country, to form the Assemblies of God in the Netherlands (*Verenigde Pinkster- en Evangeliegemeenten*, VPE; literally United Pentecostal and Evangelical Churches). This resulted in broader representation of Dutch Pentecostals in this dialogue. The last meeting was also attended by Bishop Jan van Burgsteden, spokesman for ecumenical affairs on behalf of the Dutch Roman Catholic bishops' conference.

Kees Slijkerman concluded that the goal of the dialogue's first phase was met,[34] namely 'to recognize and appreciate one another as belonging to the same Lord, to further respect and mutual understanding and to exchange the work of the Holy Spirit in each denomination'. During the eighth meeting, Hocken stressed that a dialogue with the Pentecostal movement should not follow the usual pattern of an academic comparison of mutual doctrines in an effort to reach consensus. This particular dialogue should rather 'focus on the essence of faith and Church, in line with the Second Vatican Council, (and result in) an appeal for conversion and renewal.'[35] He recognized that the dialogue in the Netherlands, which is less academic and closer to the believers, contained many elements of the model he was pleading for. He suggested to discuss the following topics in the future:

- The balance between body and spirit in faith and liturgy
- The relationship between the Word of God, the fellowship and the Holy Spirit
- Preference of scriptures to be read in the worship service
- Revival and renewal
- Contemporary eschatology

---

34. Kees Slijkerman, *Chronologisch overzicht van de eerste fase van dialoog in Nederland* (1999-2002) p. 3.
35. Press release, *Oecumenische dialoog naar een nieuw model- Achtste Dialoogdag van katholieken en pinkstergelovigen.*

GUIDELINES FOR A CHALLENGING DIALOGUE WITH PENTECOSTALS

In my dissertation of 1988, I summarized in what way a dialogue with Pentecostals[36] could be promising:

- *Liturgical creativity:* bridge the gap between body and mind
- *Social revaluation:* bridge the gap between the classes
- *Communication expertise:* bridge the gap between word and image (i.e. from a two-dimensional to a three-dimensional way of communication)
- *Intercultural exchange:* bridge the gap between cultures[37]

One could add world missions, oral and narrative theology, and more. As Pentecostals continue to grow in numbers, they can no longer hide themselves in a *fin-de-siècle* eschatology. They will be increasingly challenged about what their faith means in 'the real world' and to prove the relevance of the gifts of the Holy Spirit in society.

A prerequisite for any dialogue, particularly with Pentecostals, is that all participants are allowed and encouraged to be genuine and authentic. Let me apply this principle to the evangelistic zeal of the Pentecostal. A pastoral letter of the Netherlands Reformed Church (*Nederlands Hervormde Kerk*, NHK) stated that one has to weigh the Pentecostals instead of counting them, because a large number of them are evangelists.[38] An authentic Pentecostal will try to convert anybody who does not fit his or her perception of a reborn Christian, no matter whether the interlocutor be a liberal theologian or a Hindu. If a dialogue with Pentecostals is to succeed, one has to be ready to endure their persistent call for personal conversion, however judgmental and arrogant this may be perceived by some participants.

For their part, Pentecostals have to learn that evangelism is a dialogical process in which the evangelist too learns something about the gospel from the one he or she wants to evangelize.[39] There must be room for mutual annoyance, and it

---

36. Paul van der Laan, *The Question of Spiritual Unity*, pp. 442-447.
37. In his inventory of migrant churches in the Netherlands, Van den Broek observed: 'The most positive, well-informed reactions about pastoral and denominational integration come from the Full Gospel and Pentecostal Churches'; in A.P. van den Broek, *Ieder hoorde in zijn eigen taal*, (Amersfoort: SKIN, 2001), 7th edition, June 2001, p. 2.
38. General Synod of the Netherlands Reformed Church (Nederlandse Hervormde Kerk), *De Kerk en de Pinkstergroepen, Herderlijk Schrijven* (The Hague: Boekencentrum, 1961), p.22.
39. Walter J. Hollenweger, 'Pentecostalism, growth and ecumenism'. In: *Priest and People* (February 2003).

seems unavoidable that participants will sometimes be offended. A genuine dialogue will always be at times uncomfortable, although it may also be amusing, especially when one is confronted with the relativity of one's own persuasion. On the other hand, this dialogue should never result in a blurring of the two identities, which may produce a spiritual alien who is frightening to all concerned.

We must be prepared to listen to one another in a relational way. The Dutch queen Beatrix said in her Christmas speech of December 2002: 'Listening is more than hearing. You do not have to agree with what motivates the other in order to be open for this. To get to know someone else is a first step to a better understanding.'[40]

Based on our recent experiences in the Netherlands as described above, the following practical suggestions can be made for a fruitful ecumenical dialogue with Pentecostals:

1. All participants must have a willingness to look critically at their own tradition and be enriched by the tradition of the denomination they are in dialogue with.

2. False presuppositions and prejudices about one another must be eliminated as soon as possible. This can best be done by making an inventory of mutual perceptions in small groups during the first session. Where necessary, these perceptions can then be corrected in plenary. This often amusing exercise will also help to set the right tone for the following sessions.

3. It is essential that there be balanced participation in all elements of the dialogue: in the preparation and determination of the agenda, the number of delegates, presenters and respondents, the liturgical elements of the worship, alternate chairs of the meetings, and so on. I would also advise that the denominations take turns in hosting the meetings and vary the locations, to represent the variety of their tradition.

4. Worship and prayer should always be included in the dialogue, preferably at the beginning or end of each day. During this time, there should be room for charismatic utterances, intercession, silence and testimonies. Some may get annoyed by the noisy worship of the Pentecostals, and some Pentecostals may get upset by some liturgical elements that the other group

---

40. Christmas speech of Her Majesty Queen Beatrix, 'Onderscheid is rijkdom'. In: *Trouw* (December 27, 2002) p. 4.

introduces, but this risk must be taken. It has been our experience that all participants feel blessed and enriched by this part of the dialogue.

5. There must be a clear mutual understanding of the goal to be accomplished by the dialogue. This must regularly be evaluated and updated. The topics that are discussed should be chosen in line with the agreed goal.

6. The selection of the participants is crucial. Ideally it is a healthy balance of various ages; clergy and laity; ethnic variety and gender. All should authentically represent their denomination or tradition, doing so in an ecumenical spirit.

7. The group must be large enough to represent the various streams, but small enough for personal relationships to grow between the participants. The ideal number is probably somewhere between 20 and 30 participants.

8. The lectures and reports of the dialogue must be made accessible, preferably by publication on the internet.

Finally, what should be on the agenda for a contemporary and relevant dialogue between Pentecostals and other denominations and interest groups? In 1987, Cecil M. Robeck suggested the following six items:[41]

1. Acknowledge the universal nature of the church and allow room for one another within it.

2. Forgive and ask forgiveness of each other for the hurts we have inflicted on and received from one another.

3. Begin to treat one another as sisters and brothers, rather than as people outside the common household of faith.

4. Affirm each other's strengths and acknowledge our own weaknesses.

5. Encourage one another to live up to our expectations.

6. Undertake a mutual review of our priorities and practices to reveal helpful information.

---

41. Cecil M. Robeck, 'A proposed Pentecostal/Ecumenical Movement Dialogue Agenda'. In: *Ecumenical Trends* 16/11 (December 1987) pp. 185-188.

With hindsight, some of the suggested agenda items seem rather defensive. Never-theless, 17 years later, this agenda remains only partially fulfilled. Since Pente-costals are more doers than talkers or thinkers, I would like to add some more progressive and challenging items:

7. Realize the Biblical and universal implications of the spiritual gifts, enriched by the integration of our various denominational traditions.

8. Tackle the powers of war and injustice in this world in Jesus' name, by the power of the Holy Spirit.

9. Discover the essence of our mutual driving force.

10. Build up critical and lasting friendship.

11. Pray together for genuine and visible Christian unity.

12. Worship and celebrate together.[42]

13. Develop an ecumenical theology that integrates oral tradition and narra-tive theology.

14. Establish a community of believers from various Christian denominations, which serves as a global model of the Kingdom of God and exemplifies relevant contemporary Christianity.

15. Work out a unified plan to disciple every ethnic group according to the example of Jesus Christ.

I realize that these combined goals are rather idealistic. We surely need a specific gift of grace of the Holy Spirit to accomplish at least some of them. *Veni Creator Spiritus!*

---

42. Paul van der Laan, *The Question of Spiritual Unity*, p. 450.

9. The Challenge of Migrant Churches: Some Reflections on Theological Issues and Practical Strategies in an Unexpected Situation

Cornelis van der Kooi

The rise and spread of Pentecostal and Charismatic Christianity worldwide puts the traditional established churches in a position that in many respects requires a theological re-orientation. Elements that originate in the Pentecostal and Charismatic tradition are gradually being absorbed albeit haphazardly by the established churches. This is reflected in the field of theology. Over the years there seems to have been a shift in thinking about the Pentecostal tradition from outright rejection to critical openness.[1]

The need for a re-orientation, however, becomes all the more urgent when traditional churches (which in sociological and cultural terms also find themselves in a minority situation) are confronted with a vital Pentecostal Christianity that is of non-Western origin. This is the situation that exists in some of the larger cities in the Netherlands, such as Amsterdam, with a relatively high percentage of non-Western migrants. In many ways, this entails a new situation for the existing churches and their predominant theology.

---

1. Regarding the caution of the Reformed world, see for example the very characteristic paper by Carver T.Yu, 'Charismatic Movement, Postmodernism, and Covenantal Rationality' and Myung Yong Kim, 'Reformed Pneumatology and Pentecostal Pneumatology'. In: Wallace M. Alston, Jr./ Michael Welker, *Reformed Theology: Identity and Ecumenicity* (Grand Rapids/Cambridge: Eerdmans, 2003) pp. 157-169 and 170-189. By contrast, the reactions of some Netherlands theologians of the Dutch Reformed tradition are much more positive, such as K. Runia, *Op zoek naar de Geest* (Kampen: Kok, 2000) and C. Graafland, *Gereformeerden op zoek naar God. Godsverduistering in het licht van de gereformeerde spiritualiteit* (Kampen: De Groot Goudriaan, 1990). In the Netherlands, the ecumenical *Charismatische Werkgemeenschap Nederland* (Ecumenical Charismatic Renewal of the Netherlands, CWN) has done much to foster openness and to show interest. The most important members of the movement are K.J. Kraan, W. Verhoef, W.C. Verdam, N. van Ditmarsch, M.F.G. Parmentier and J. Veenhof.

The purpose of this article is to present some observations about this new situation and the challenge that this gives rise to, as well as to point out issues that call for more detailed theological reflection.

A New Situation

To begin with, I should first underline the limited scope of this contribution of mine. The observations and comments that follow are no more than a provisional commentary on the present situation of the churches in the Netherlands. Their main purpose is to raise awareness. They are not at all intended to be a definitive or comprehensive discussion of the issues involved. At the same time, it seems to me that what I am advancing here will *mutatis mutandis* likely also apply to situations encountered elsewhere in modern Western cities and societies.

The churches in the Netherlands and the various theological movements that are predominant within these churches, find themselves confronted with forms of Christianity and the Christian faith that they are not familiar with and which they in many respects find strange as regards faith in practice, preaching, leading a life of faith. In terms of theology, these are at odds with what is acceptable within the established churches. The large churches have by now grown used to the sheer fact of the Pentecostal churches' existence, and conversations with the Pentecostal denomination have gotten underway albeit with many hesitations, even reluctance.

In the Netherlands, it is thanks to the Charismatic movement within the large established churches that one can speak of a cautious acceptance of Pentecostal and Charismatic Christianity. Certainly, the cautious conversation between the Pentecostal groups and the traditional churches, as well as the gradual growth of a Charismatic movement within the churches themselves, have not yet changed much in terms of the existing theological relations. It could however be – and I deliberately choose my words carefully – that the advent of foreign churches whose religious life is predominantly Pentecostal, causes the traditional churches and theology to again re-examine their own identity. One can think of enough reasons that make such an encounter desirable and even necessary. Given the limited space within cities, both groups can hardly avoid each other and in some respects they find themselves in the same situation. The existing churches are just as much a minority within urban society as the new groups of foreigners, albeit that their experience of 'otherness' will certainly be very different.

For sure, the sociological and social starting-point is very different. Whereas the existing indigenous churches have undergone a painful process of loss of sociological and cultural dominance, the lot of the new groups of foreigners is that of being cultural and social newcomers. For the latter, the struggle to become familiar with a new country, with another climate and another set of rules, on top of the struggle for economic survival, goes hand in hand with the challenge to lead a life of faith in God and to propagate it in this new context. However, in terms of their religious practice and background, they represent what is currently the largest and fastest-growing part of Christianity worldwide. The indigenous churches in Europe and most Western theologians are barely aware of this new situation.

In this context, I want to recall something said by Walter J. Hollenweger. He contends that it is high time for European theology to focus on the new global relationships, if it does not want 'to descend to the level of being the ideology of some West and Central European tribes'.[2] I am convinced that this does not mean that the Western churches have to start imitating the religious life of the migrant churches or to view them as setting a new standard against which to measure their own spiritual life. That would be nonsense and likely to end up in a grandiose fiasco. What I mean is that the manner in which Christian faith was shaped in another culture, be recognized as a mirror by means of which one can ask oneself what it is that one has to learn about oneself.

THE (UN)OBVIOUSNESS OF MODERNITY

This brings me to an issue that, in so far as I can see, has scarcely been recognised as an issue and a challenge. The challenge lies in the fact that Western Christians are confronted at close quarters with a Christianity that does not bear the hallmarks of modernity and which for that very reason deviates in all sorts of ways from what is familiar in terms of ecclesiology and theology. That does not in itself have to be seen as a bad thing, were it not for the strong identification of Western theology with modern culture. The Western churches have been shaped culturally and theologically by modernity. What is more, one has to ask whether modernity is not in fact viewed by present-day Western theology as the form that is most profoundly normative for every form of (tenable) Christian faith. Or has the Western self-assurance not come to this?

We will have to bear in mind that there is a difference between theory and practice. The theory may state that modernity is not due the status given to it, whereas practical experience may show otherwise. For Western theology it is clear: the history of theology over the last two centuries can be described as an attempt to

---

2. W.J. Hollenweger, *Charismatisch-pfingstliches Christentum. Herkunft, Situation, ökumenische Praxis* (Göttingen: Vandenhoeck und Ruprecht, 1997) p. 16.

keep pace with a culture in which the human person's value as subject of his or her world gains in importance. Standing up for one's rights in the face of autocratically governing authorities becomes a value that is increasingly laid down in civil rights and constitutions. This process has also influenced religious belief.

In the process of differentiating and rationalising life, theology has done its utmost to develop theory that counters the decline of religiosity, sometimes by qualifying these processes as a lamentable loss, but usually by arguing them to be a necessary consequence of the removal of the divine from the world, by means of which the *seculum* finally gains its rightful independence. The theologian Karl Barth is well known for his very critical stance on modernity. He ventured to describe the history of Protestant theology as a process of decline. But even in his case, one can at least detect an ambivalence that, when it does matter, wants to locate the process of modernisation within a learning process which, thanks to divine providence, has befallen the church.[3]

Seen in cultural terms, the Pentecostal migrant churches are outsiders. The Western values of modernity are not part and parcel of the cultural background to their religious life. Instead, they bring their African or Asian context with them and have to be understood in that light. The African context, by the way, again reminds us of the roots of the Pentecostal movement that spread in the 20th century. It should never be forgotten that much of Pentecostalism has a non-European, African background. This is due to William Seymour, the black preacher who led the Azusa Street revival in 1906 and launched Pentecostalism as a movement that overcame the barriers between races and classes, women and men.[4] The presence of non-Western migrant churches is therefore a living reminder of that background and the new co-existence provides a theological agenda for various fields of theology. This theological agenda is of fundamental importance.

If a fruitful relationship between these churches is not just to be a gesture of goodwill, then differences really do have to be faced and made a ground for self-reflection. Not that Westerners can or have to immediately lay aside their own culture. Again, this would be foolish. In this respect, it is – theologically speaking – important to postulate the thesis of God's freedom. In making himself known to humans, God is not exclusively bound up with a particular culture. Human

---

3. Karl Barth, *Kirchliche Dogmatik IV/3* (Zollikon, Zürich: Evangelische Verlag, 1967) p. 40.
4. Hollenweger, *Charismatisch-pfingstliches Christentum*, p. 32. A. Anderson, *An Introduction to Pentecostalism: Global Charismatic Christianity* (Cambridge, UK: Cambridge University Press, 2004) p. 43.

knowledge of God never results from particular cultural conditions. God can make himself known in various cultural circumstances.

The fundamental theological thesis on divine revelation is of great importance so as to be able to appraise each appropriation of the Christian faith and relate it to God's turning [toward humankind through Christ Jesus]. But that also means that various forms of appropriation can form a mirror for the other. What does God want us to learn from what we see mirrored in others? When this question is not posed and the theological confrontation is avoided, then the contact with the migrant churches degenerates into mere Asian or African folklore. In the following paragraphs I want to mention a few points for reflection.

DEALING WITH THE BIBLE

Contemporary theology has grown used to the view that the critical way in which it deals with the Bible and with Christian tradition, actually sets the standard for sound theology. The non-Western migrant churches confront this with theological assumptions that are in fact at odds with this view. The theology of the Western churches is very much determined by the question about the truth of human knowledge of God, and dealing with the Bible as a literary given begins with an initial distance to the biblical text as being a foreign text.

By contrast, the Pentecostal non-Western churches actually live within an oral culture in which the historical-critical or literary-critical ways of dealing with the Bible are not dominant. Instead, the biblical stories and images are part and parcel of one's own experience of God's presence in everyday life. Each believer with his or her testimony forms part of the story; and the appropriation of what is heard is not a last step, but a supposition that is predetermined. One is oneself part of the drama presented in the biblical story.

THE (NON-)SELF-EVIDENCE OF GOD

This difference is noticeable in all sorts of areas, not least when dealing with the question as to who or what is God. For the churches in the West, God is no longer self-evident. In their churches, God is talked about with much hesitation and caution. There too, in a post-modern context, the importance of stories and one's own life-story is being discovered. But when a Western theologian speaks, it is above all the human being who tells his or her own life-story and thereby is the subject that designs his or her own world. This differs from the migrant churches, where a similar state of reflection on one's own subjectivity is completely absent. On the contrary, the decisive actor is God himself, or Jesus who directly intervenes and is active in the present.

This contrast not only characterises the difference in climate and atmosphere. It also points to a very important difference in theological assumption. In Western theology, God is spoken about in terms of his being hidden or even absent. The Pentecostal tradition starts out from the assumption that God is present, as is the Spirit who is active and will come, even when the present is marked by suffering and pain. In short, the historical churches feel theologically ill at ease with a theology whose contents they associate with an orthodoxy from which they have grown apart. For their part, the migrant churches had expected more 'pious' churches in the West and, to their surprise, find themselves in a situation of neo-paganism.

One can ask oneself what the next step should or must be. Is the next step that the migrant churches gradually familiarize themselves with the paradigm of post-modernity and that, given the new cultural and theological climate, the self-evidence of belief in God of itself becomes tainted by corrosion? Does Western theology really set the standard and is it just a matter of tenacity to get the foreign churches to avow those values and norms that are predominant in the mainstream of modern Protestantism? That would be a case of huge arrogance and could point to the fact that colonialism remains alive and kicking, at least in the field of theology. Or could it be that the terms 'pre-modern' and 'modern' are grossly inadequate and actually offer Pentecostal Christianity cause to reflect once more in detail about the self-evidence of its own post-modernity? That is what I suspect.

THE STATUS OF JESUS

The status of Jesus is one of the issues on the theological agenda of modern Christianity in the West. For most migrant churches and groups of the Pentecostal tradition, the status of Jesus is fundamental. The significance of Jesus Christ as someone who lives and acts in the present, as Son of God, is brought to the fore in all shades and varieties by means of testimonies and hymns. From the viewpoint of modern Christianity, it is precisely these churches that are at great risk of being guilty of Jesuology. Only Jesus, not God the Father, is invoked. It is no longer about God being the one who forms the mystery of Jesus' mission and calling, but only about Jesus as human being who is God.

There is great uncertainty and discord in Western churches on matters of Christology. Is Jesus the exponent of God's kingdom? Or does he, in his life and dying, also form the basis and entry-point for a new relationship with God? Western theology currently seems to have a strong preference for a pneumatological approach regarding Jesus. Jesus proceeds from God's Spirit. He is, in fact, a figure who is called into being by the Spirit of God. And the church lives by means of the same Spirit in which Jesus had lived. But to what extent Jesus is God's Spirit made visible, or whether he is God made visible, in whose absence one can no longer think about God, is an important question that often remains unresolved.

The various positions that are held on Christology seem to be anything but academic matters. The theological position that one holds in this regard is immediately apparent in how one prays and worships. Who is being addressed? Whenever it is God the Father who is addressed, does this also include Jesus? If, in the wake of having arisen and ascended, he is part of God's rule, then there is reason to address him, to honour him – in keeping with the liturgy of the last book of the Bible – as Alpha and Omega, to whom all power is given. If, on the other hand, the person of Jesus in fact ended his existence with the death on the cross, and the images of being raised and of ascension can only be understood as a metaphorical use of language that does not refer to Jesus the person living together with God the Father, then it is impossible to address him directly in prayer.

WHAT IS 'MISSIO DEI'?

The preceding remarks about the status of Jesus and his significance in Christian belief is directly linked with the following: What is the content of the church's message? What is its mission? If there is to be a form of cooperation between migrant churches and the traditional churches, then there has to be a real exchange and, if necessary, confrontation about this point. The content of the preaching that one can hear in Pentecostal migrant churches is often extremely clear, for many indigenous Christians even somewhat too clear and concrete.

Distinctions are made in black-and-white terms, between a life in darkness under the sway of dark powers, and life in the light, under the rule of Jesus and the Spirit. The powers and expressions of evil are referred to in concrete terms and, if necessary, forcefully cast out in Jesus' name. The devil is an objective entity and liberation from the devil's power takes place with many onlookers. There seems to be no need for a hermeneutical treatment and development of the linguistic landscape of the Gospels.

At first sight, there seems to be complete continuity between the world of the New Testament and the present. One of Rudolf Bultmann's *bon mots* was that whoever turns on the electric light with the flick of a switch, can no longer unflinchingly suppose the world of the New Testament to be the prevailing standard. The religious life of many Pentecostal migrant churches will most likely cause those who are familiar with Bultmann's *bon mot* to desperately ask themselves whether the chasm between their own religious life and that of the migrant churches can still be filled.

However, the likely despair concerns not only the symbolic world in which the message is brought. The symbolic world is inextricably interwoven with the message. And so the question arises: what is the redemption? What actually is the 'missio Dei'?[5] From what does the world need to be liberated? What is the liberation of humans? Does the Church's mission concur with humanity, the true humanity whereby each human being can grow and blossom as a person in his or her own right, who responds to God by being a partner in his kingdom? And to what extent are the ideals of the Western world, with their vision of the dignity and freedom of the human being, implicitly or even explicitly identified with the message of the kingdom?

I want it to be clear that in raising these questions, I do not wish to suggest that we have to regress with regard to humans being able to stand up for their rights and the value of the human person. Those are elements that in the history of modernity are heavily contested in hierarchical cultures, in which each human is completely subjugated to the will and dictate of an autocratic ruler. But where the notion of this maturity becomes independent, one can ascertain the disappearance of the community's value as an association where the human person emerges, gains his or her place and in a certain sense remains dependent.

And so the question remains as to the content of the message of the kingdom. The discussion about the 'missio Dei' that to this day is being conducted in mission circles, seems also to be highly topical in the confrontation with the migrant churches. The discussion features two mutually opposing positions. The first stance holds that the 'missio Dei' intends the humanisation of existence. That is why, according to this conception of the 'missio Dei', the struggle for a more just society, the fight against poverty, against racism, against discrimination and globalism, can be waged and supported in terms of mission as the common denominator.

The second stance holds that the 'missio Dei' is, above all, a matter of faith and conversion, a reversal in which the response is to God's turning [to humankind through Jesus Christ] and practical steps are taken to effect the sanctification of one's own life. Talk about the social context is secondary. It is patently obvious and urgently necessary that this antagonism be overcome by a stance in which both elements, the personal and the social, are fully acknowledged.[6]

---

5. See the special theme issue of *Weltmission Heute* 52 (2003), titled 'Missio Dei Heute', published by the Association of Protestant Churches and Missions in Germany (EMW). Regarding the development and history of the concept of *missio Dei*, see in particular the article by Tormod Engelsviken, pp. 35-57.
6. See Theo Sundermaier's proposal in *Weltmission Heute* 52 (2003), pp. 147-171.

THE SLAVE'S YOKE OF ACADEMIC DIFFERENTIATION

It is not my intention, given the brevity of this article, to repeat and continue the discussion about the content of the 'missio Dei'. However, it is of great importance to establish that these issues are not limited to the field of missiology and only of importance to a world far removed from us. The issues in this field and the timidity are entirely theological. That is to say, biblical studies, dogmatics, missiology, theology or intercultural theology cannot each deal with this theme by themselves. It is high time that theologians realize that the differentiation of theology in specialist disciplines often acts as a slave's yoke that does not do justice to the unity of life. Only when, in dealing with these issues, we go back to the biblical accounts and are ready to learn from these anew the various connotations of the biblical concept of God's kingdom, is there a chance that the old stalemate will be overcome. Above all, what must be prevented is Western theologians claiming to be the only ones who can point out where the gods of this century are hiding or boldly reveal themselves.

PRACTICAL STRATEGIES

How can church and theology really open themselves for encounter and confrontation with the migrant churches? Which strategies might it be worth considering? I first name a very practical example that can be developed locally. Migrant churches should be shown practical hospitality by offering them premises for worship or by helping them find such premises. Such hospitality involves offering to help in making contact with local authorities, district councils and estate agents. There is currently an initiative to provide places of worship started by the Evangelical Working Alliance. It deserves every support from churches, church social services and individuals.

Besides this, the theological training institutes should accept their responsibility and develop opportunities for further training of clergy and church leaders. This is, of course, no simple matter, given that differences in preparatory training and practical opportunities for study are often obstructive factors, but this does not lessen the need to undertake initiatives. Above all, it offers the opportunity to develop a form of putting theology into practice that is not just a matter of the head, but that combines head with heart.

THE NECESSITY OF A PNEUMATOLOGICAL RE-ORIENTATION

The influence of Pentecostal Christianity on Western churches has already for some considerable time been noticeable because of the steady increase of Charismatic elements in church life. An example in the Netherlands is the Ecumenical Charismatic Renewal in the Netherlands (CWN), which has done tremendous pioneering work for the larger churches. The CWN has convinced many that one does not have to leave the established church to take the work of the Spirit seriously, but that devotion to the Spirit's work and renewal of spiritual life fits in every respect within an ecumenical embedment.[7]

In the meantime, devotion to the work and gifts of the Spirit has developed distinct forms in countless places. Ecclesiastical as well as theological re-orientation is occurring, albeit hesitantly, in the area of pneumatology. In the first place there is, of course, the Catholic Charismatic Renewal which, as part of the Roman Catholic Church, can benefit as no other from being an international church and thereby having an international network. In a small country such as the Netherlands, we also see all sorts of initiatives in smaller churches, such as the New Wine movement, which very much draws on the legacy of John Wimber's ideas. We see the emergence of youth churches and cautious experimenting with customs and traditions that have their place in Charismatic renewal, such as more spacious premises for praise and healing services.

I mention these elements because they can serve as stepping-stones in the contact with and understanding for the migrant churches. In other words, Western historical Christianity has to learn that the New Testament not only talks about salvation in terms of saving souls and that the kingdom is not tantamount to a social-ethical programme. Salvation and preservation also imply healing and salvation in a broader sense. Both these elements – namely the fact that the Gospel has a message that conveys a sense of feeling safe with God and that combines with salvific actions – both have once again to be rehabilitated. The established Western churches should listen and learn, among other, from the migrant churches, how for them healing and salvation go together. In one way or another, form has to be given to the congregation as a salvific community. For Christian theology, also in its academic form, this can result in a re-orientation of its content and function, as seen from the pneumatological perspective.

---

7. On the current state of affairs, see the jubilee issue of the *Bulletin voor Charismatische Theologie* 50 (2002), which contains articles, among other, by R. van Elderen, J. van der Veken, R. van Kooij, S. Stoppels, C. van der Kooi, J. Veenhof and M.F.G. Parmentier.

10. Intermezzo – The Adventure of Faith: Some Pictures from Matthew and Luke[1]

Walter J. Hollenweger

The Missiologist Matthew

Matthew ends his Gospel with the famous great commission: 'Go ye therefore and make disciples of all nations, baptizing them, *teaching them to observe all things I have commanded you...*'

On the basis of these two verses, many Americans and Europeans have gone into the Third World in order to convince the pagans of their error. However, they unfortunately did not read the text exactly. What does the text command the disciples? *'To teach the nations to observe all things I (Jesus) have commanded you.'* And what has Jesus commanded his disciples? Did he teach them that he, Jesus, was the Son of God, that he was true God and true man? No, of course not.

Jesus was – at least according to Matthew – not interested in his own ontology, in a metaphysics about himself. He taught his disciples to love God and their neighbour as they loved themselves. He gave examples of that in the sermon on the mount, in his parables and through the example of his life; for instance, that he rather preferred to suffer injustice than to do injustice. According to Matthew's great commission, our christological elaborations (such as his atoning death and other later theories) are not part of his mission.

Furthermore, Matthew begins his Gospel with the story of the astrologers. These pagan astrologers from Baghdad were not kings, as Christian legend later made them out to be. They were pagan astrologers who found the way to the cradle on the basis of an evangelistic sermon by a missionary; the 'Bible-reading' scribes in Jerusalem were engaged in a plot to kill the infant Jesus.

---

1. This article was published earlier as 'Intercultural Theology: Some Remarks on the Term', in: M. Frederiks e.a., *Towards an Intercultural Theology: Essays in Honour of Jan A.B. Jongeneel*, Zoetermeer: Boekencentrum 2003, p. 89-97.

It is fairly obvious that this story is a theological parable, just like the parables of Jesus. Nobody asks: Was there ever a father with two sons? Was there ever a landowner who paid all his workers the same wage? Was there ever a widow who put her last dime in the collection-box? Was there ever a woman who prepared the dough for baking bread? Jesus and the authors of the Gospel taught theology by stories. Therefore, the question of the historical authenticity of this passage is beside the point, a conclusion that evangelical theologians – not only so-called liberals – have reached long ago (for example James Dunn).

Of course, there are other passages that explicitly want to be historical. That is why we study theology in order to distinguish between these different genres of literature. But in this piece of narrative theology, Matthew wants to teach his congregation: Pagans too have something important to contribute to the Gospel. Theologically speaking, they are not empty potato-bags. After all, Matthew probably lived in the multi-religious city of Antioch. For him and for all authors of the New Testament, it was self-evident that the non-Christian religions were not only erroneous. They too contributed to truth.

Imagine if Mary had been a Pentecostal pastor's wife. Here come the foreign astrologers with their frightening signs of the zodiac on their garments. Certainly, she would have said: 'You pagan foreigners, you occultists. Do not come near my baby. You might put a curse on him. Go away!' Fortunately she was a Jewish mother and so she said: 'Gentlemen, come near! See my baby.' And so they came near and brought gold, myrrh and frankincense, as signs of their pagan culture and religion.

There are other passages in the New Testament that show respect for pagan religions. Take for instance Matthew 15.21ff. Here a pagan woman comes to Jesus and asks him to heal her daughter. But Jesus does not even answer her. His disciples say to him: 'Send her away, for she keeps shouting after us.' But Jesus – according to this passage – behaves in a way that, seen from today's standpoint, can only be described as racist. He says: 'I am only sent to the Jews. I shall have nothing to do with this pagan woman. It is not fair to take the bread from the table of the children and throw it to the dogs.' Jesus was a Jew, so he compares Jews with children and pagans with dogs. (Sorry, I did not write the Gospel of Matthew).

Instead of being angry at Jesus, the woman kneels before him and says: 'Yes, but dogs receive the crumbs that fall from the table of their master.' And here the miracle happens. Jesus is healed from his racism by the intervention of the pagan woman. He learns something about his own ministry from a pagan woman. And so he heals her daughter. This is an extraordinary story, for Jesus, the Son of

God, learns something from a pagan woman. Therefore we, his disciples, can perhaps also learn something from this pagan woman. Who are we to think we can learn nothing from the pagans.

Thesis no. 1: God speaks to us through pagans. In fact, many become Christians via a detour, for instance via yoga or forms of esoteric religion or even via Marxism. Sometimes the detour is the direct way.

THE MISSIOLOGIST LUKE

Most people think that mission, education, proclamation is the transfer of religious information from a knowledgeable person (a professor, a missionary, a pastor) to those who are ignorant.

This type of mission only produces copies of the professor, the missionary, the pastor. These copies are not viable and can only survive with subsidies from those who are interested in the survival of their own copies. This is the understanding of education in many of our schools and universities, and of mission in many of our churches. Unfortunately it has very little in common with the understanding of mission in the New Testament.
Take the story of Peter and Cornelius, which is usually called 'the conversion of Cornelius'. It could just as well be called 'the conversion of Peter'. This Lukan piece of narrative theology presents a totally different picture of mission.

Cornelius knew something about God and salvation before he was evangelized by Peter. Mission in this context means that Peter and Cornelius exchange their understanding of and their experience with God. In the course of this evangelism, Cornelius does not become a copy of Peter. He becomes a Christian who was different from Peter. A new type of Christian emerges. In contrast to the Jewish Christian Peter, Cornelius becomes a Hellenistic Christian; that is to say, a Christian who does not observe the Sabbath nor circumcision. He does not go to the temple, and he does not follow the Jewish food regulations.

And Peter accepts this new type of Christianity. He even baptizes Cornelius. But Peter himself does not become a Hellenistic Christian. He continues to observe the Sabbath, circumcision, the Jewish food taboos. But he does not demand the same from Cornelius. Cornelius develops his own type of Christianity, different from Peter's. He does not become a copy of Peter. And this is the basis of Christian ecumenism and Christian tolerance. Studying the history of mission, it is astonishing how many Christian missionaries and teachers want to create copies of themselves.

If Cornelius had not developed a new type of Christianity, Christianity would have remained a small Jewish reform sect. Because it overcame the frontiers between the Jewish and the Hellenistic cultures, it became a universal religion. That Hellenistic Christianity later became the majority Christianity and persecuted the original Jewish Christianity, killing all those who disagreed with it, is one of the tragedies of Christian mission history.[2]

Crossing the frontiers of culture has happened several times since; for instance, when Christianity overcame the frontiers between the Greek and the Roman worlds, and between the Roman and the Germanic worlds. Each time, Christianity was fundamentally changed. Theology, liturgy and ethics were changed. This is also happening in our own times, when Christianity overcomes the frontiers between our Mediterranean culture and the Chinese, the African, the Indonesian cultures.

Each time, a new type of Christianity emerges with new questions, with new forms of worship, with new theologies. This is particularly clear in Africa and in China, which never have been touched by Aristotelian philosophy. There is a fundamental difference between these cultures and the Western ones. These transformations of Christianity are necessary if the Christian church is to survive.

Now, you will say to me: Hang on, that is not true. It is only the outward form, not the kernel of Christianity, that is changed. The content does not change, only the packaging. By arguing like this, you think that you can distinguish between form and content, which is in itself an Aristotelian form of arguing. This type of arguing is foreign to the biblical authors.

The leaders in Jerusalem argued with Peter like this: 'What has happened to you, Peter? Of course, we know that you have always been emotional. But what you did here, is going much too far. You fraternize with an officer of the Roman occupation army. You eat unclean food, which God has prohibited thousands of years ago. It makes us sick, even to think of the unclean snails, crabs and other terrible food you have eaten.

'Furthermore, you have fellowship with a pagan. Yea, you even baptized him without making sure that he understood the Gospel in the same way as we do. Where will it all lead to, if suddenly the reliable and proven apostles – these pillars of tradition in Jerusalem – are no longer the unquestionable authority in the

---

2. See in detail on this: *Petrus, der Pontifex* (Kindhausen, Switzerland: Metanoia, 2003), with music and choreography.

church? Peter, you have betrayed the Lord already once. You risk doing the same again. Will you ever learn?'

What did Peter reply to these charges? He simply said: 'I had a vision.' Well, try that with your church authorities. In the case of Peter and the apostles in Jerusalem, the biblical record says – and that is the miracle of the story – 'When the apostles heard this, they became silent and praised God, saying: Also the pagans may be saved.'

Thesis no. 2: Mission (education, proclamation, evangelism) is a two-way process. The missionary (evangelist, teacher, pastor) learns from those he wants to evangelize, as they do from him. I, for my part, have learned more from my students than from anybody else.

CONCLUSION

What does mission mean according to Luke and Matthew? It means: We have to move away from our petrified forms of theology, of worship, of evangelism, into new forms of theology and mission. And that is exactly what is happening in Amsterdam. The Azusa Pentecostal Bible College moved onto the campus of the Free University of Amsterdam. Nobody can tell what that means for the university – and for the Pentecostals.

Being a Christian theologian, a missionary, means to be constantly surprised by the Holy Spirit. I have experienced that myself. I started my Christian pilgrimage as a Pentecostal evangelist in a rather narrow-minded Swiss Pentecostal church. And because the Lord blessed my work, I got into contact with other Christians. The Lord moved me out into the ecumenical movement, into university life. And at each turning of the way, I met one or several Corneliuses who were or who became Christians of a very different type.

And now, toward the end of my life, the different strands come together again, the ecumenical form of Christianity, the academic and the Pentecostal variety of being a Christian. No longer do we need to fight each other. Isn't that something wonderful?[3]

---

3. More on this by Lynne Price, *Theology Out of Place. A Theological Biography of Walter J. Hollenweger* (London: Sheffield Academic Press, 2002).

III   MINISTRY OF HEALING

11. Churches as Healing Communities: Impulses from the South for an Integral Understanding of Healing

Wout van Laar

No one who is interested in global ecumenism and mission can miss it: Healing is high on the churches' agenda. In May 2005, the World Mission Conference of the World Council of Churches took place in Athens, with as its theme 'Come, Holy Spirit, heal and reconcile'.[1] Earlier, in 2003, the Conference of European Churches held its assembly in Trondheim, the title of which was 'Jesus Christ heals and reconciles'.[2]

In that same year, Santiago de Chile was the venue of an inspiring consultation on the relationship between healing and mission. The consultation was jointly organised by the Latin American Council of Churches and the World Council, to prepare for 'Athens'. For the first time, Pentecostal Christians were by far in the majority, so that they could make their mark on the gathering. Times have changed. The powerful trumpet of liberation theology is no longer being heard. The Gospel is now above all understood as a force for healing and reconciliation. Testimonies showed how many find the way of discipleship through healing, to themselves or to friends or neighbours. 'Lord, I have no money for a doctor, but I know you as a God who is alive and who saves.'

The letter to the churches which was drawn up at the end of the meeting, issued a call to the churches: let us recognise that the service of healing is an integral part of the proclamation of the Gospel. One could detect a sense of determination among the participants to dedicate themselves wherever possible to 'healing communities' at the grass-roots level, in slums and in rural areas. Places of hope

---

1. For the preparatory consultations in Ghana (2002) and Chile (2003), see 'Divine Healing, Pentecostalism and Mission'. In: *International Review of Mission*, vol. 93., nos. 370/371 (July/October 2004). More recent information is available at the World Mission Conference's website, www.mission2005.org.
2. Assembly XII, Trondheim 2003, Final Report, CEC Geneva. See also Keith Clements, The Churches in Europe as Witnesses to Healing (Geneva: 2003).

amid countless forms of pain and brokenness, where God can be encountered and experienced as Healer.[3]

One can point to at least five causes for this broad interest in what in international discussions is called healing. This summary list highlights how many aspects there are to the subject.

1. It is being put on the agenda by the churches of the South, which are gaining in significance. The ministry of healing usually forms a regular part of church life, not just in the independent and Pentecostal churches, but also in the more traditional churches in Africa, Latin America and Asia.

2. New Age influences and all manner of forms of new religiosity cause there to be increased awareness of a more 'holistic' approach. It involves the whole human being in all of his or her relations. The human being is seen as a psychosomatic unit.

3. The craving for wholeness exists everywhere. Awareness of brokenness and of the darker sides of human existence leads people to seek the inner path.[4] In so doing, they come up against the limitations of materialism, individualism and a career-oriented lifestyle.

4. There are critical views on the role of churches in recent ethnic conflicts. How can the church make a positive contribution in processes of reconciliation in areas such as Rwanda and the Balkans? In this context, the issues have to do with forgiveness and retribution, restitution and 'healing of memories'.

5. The tragedy of AIDS compels the churches throughout the world to work out their role in the fight against this terrible epidemic that disrupts entire societies.

It is not easy to find a Dutch translation that does justice to all the nuances of the concept 'healing'. It evokes both the notion of healing ['genezing'] and of sal-

---

3. 'Geloof, heelmaking en zending' [Faith, healing and mission]. Consultation jointly organised by CLAI and WCC in Santiago de Chile, October 28-31, 2003. Report [in Dutch] by Wout van Laar available from the NZR. For the complete text, see *International Review of Mission, ibid.*, pp. 407 ff.
4. See *Hunkering naar heelheid. Het nieuw-religieuze verlangen naar een authentiek bestaan.* A brochure [in Dutch] of the working-group on new religious movements of the Catholic Council for Church and Society ('s-Hertogenbosch: October 2000).

vation ['heil']. In the German ('Heil' and 'Heilung'), the connection between salvation and healing is immediately apparent. On the other hand, placing the Dutch
terms 'heil' and 'heling' next to each other, produces impossible associations.[5]
'Heelmaken' [mending; literally 'making whole'] sounds better.

Wholeness ['heelheid'] gets us to think of physical health as well as spiritual and
social well-being. After all, the human being cannot merely be viewed as a self-
contained individual, but as a being who comes into her or his own in community with others, with nature and with God. In the end, it is about the restored
relations with God, with one's fellow human being, with oneself. That is why the
church is oriented towards the salvation ['heil'], the healing ['heelwording',
becoming whole] of the entire world.[6]

The Netherlands Missionary Council wrote in 2002 a publication with the aim
of getting the discussion going in its home country [i.e. the Netherlands].[7] The
publication provides resources on how to get started on the theme of healing,
above all practically-minded and together: as 'Ecumenicals' and 'Evangelicals',
as Roman Catholics and Pentecostals, as white and black Christians.

Perhaps this publication can be seen as preparatory material to the World Mission Conference. But above all, it is about one's own society. That is where developments occur that seriously damage the wholeness of the human being and that
in many ways cause one physically, socially and spiritually to become sick.

On the one hand, we are living in a time of great welfare, despite the present stag-
nation in economic growth. On the other hand, many people are weighed down
by many forms of brokenness. There is a sense of insecurity in our risk society,
fear of the implications of a multicultural society and uneasiness about bureaucratic and political complacency. The complexity of this situation causes many
'doctors of society' to groan: what is the matter? How can we get the patient back
to health?
Churches share in this sense of confusion. However, they also realize that they
have the task of being present in ways that bring healing to the many forms of
brokenness. In this situation, it is of crucial importance to reach a deeper understand of the calling of the church regarding the ministry of healing. Can our congregations and parishes renew themselves as hospitable and healing communities,

---

5. 'heling' can mean either 'healing' or 'receiving stolen goods'.
6. Martien Parmentier, *Heil maakt heel. De bediening tot genezing* (Meinema, 1997) p.
   13.
7. *Volgelingen van de Wounded Healer. De zending van de kerk in de dienst van genezing.*
   Included in the annual report 2000/2001 (Amsterdam, 2002).

where the liberating presence of Jesus as Saviour is experienced as new? And is there also room for healing practices and liturgies that give this a well-considered form?

In this article, we turn to the churches of the South to find out about the distinctive way in which the churches there go about healing. It is worth the effort to gather in-depth knowledge of the insights and intuitions from Africa and Latin America. Healing as practised by Jesus is closer to the everyday life of non-Western Christians than for us children of the Enlightenment. This is apparent from a renewed reading of the first chapters of the gospel according to Matthew, with which this contribution concludes.

THE HEALING CHURCHES OF THE SOUTH

In Western society, medicine is practised in the hospital, religion in the church. In Africa, matters are different. Healing is an integral part of church life in the Third World. But what is very distinctive is the central role of healing in the independent African 'healing churches'.

Father Verstraelen tells of how, in 1965, he first came into contact with this phenomenon:

> They were small, independent Christian groups which, with the Bible in the hand, made claim to share in the healing power of Christ. Catholic and Protestant churches found these to be primitive goings-on. After all, they themselves had hospitals and clinics where people were treated with modern medical insights and means. What the members of these churches did not know was that their members went with their complaints and troubles to gatherings of these healing churches.[8]

The missionary aura of these healing churches and other charismatic movements has since then only increased. In conjunction with ancient African traditions, they know Christ as the healing medicine-man. They show a holistic view of healing and health that is far removed from that of the Westerners with their faith in the Enlightenment: illness not only affects the individual, but is experienced as rupture and disturbance of the state of equilibrium. It is a matter of restoring the cohesion of things. Nature and society are also involved. Things are little different in the indigenous cultures of Latin America and Asia.

---

8. Frans Verstraelen, *Gerechtigheid eenheid en vrede* (Amersfoort: De Horsting, 1982), quoted by Robert van Essen, Heel de stad. De christelijke gemeente als 'wounded healer', doctoral thesis on missiology, Amsterdam 1996, p. 32.

It is important to discern the more deep-seated causes of suffering, illness and death of many millions of people in our age: the frightening gulf between rich and poor. The unjust distribution of wealth means injustice and premature death for huge numbers of people. A new subproletariat of uprooted generations migrate from the rural areas to continually expanding illegal settlements around the metropolises in Africa, Latin America and Eurasia. They are written off by the economic system. Without work, without access to medical care and education, without rights, they wage a daily struggle for survival. It is precisely in these situations of exclusion and pain, that new forms of faith are now coming into existence, forms previously unknown to us. While the rich part of the world has declared God dead, poor people in situations of brokenness experience that – to their surprise – God is in their midst, healing and liberating.

Harvey Cox, professor of Religion at Harvard University speaks of God's revenge on secularisation.[9] He perceives an almost universal sense of homelessness. Whether middle-class or poor, by the last decades of the 20th century more and more people in every part of the world felt uprooted and spiritually homeless.

> Whether it was poverty or geographical dislocation or cultural chaos that caused it, all sensed the loss of a secure place in a world where whirl was king.[10]

Thus healing communities come into being in an age when the old order seems to be falling apart and the new order is not yet visible. They offer a safe haven where you can tell your stories of distress and healing, where you can share problems and pain without being judged; a place where you can ask others to pray for your healing and strength to persevere; a place where you can ask for help without money or particular rituals being preconditions. In healing communities, people find a new home, rediscover their dignity and create for themselves the space that others denied them. That experience inspires to share the little that one has with others. The effects of this are continued in the broader social context. Could it be that the Spirit is actively engaged in the crisis of our age to create something new, starting out from the margins of the world? Can what is growing there perhaps be of significance for our common future, for the very survival of humankind?[11]

Churches in the West do not seem able to become sufficiently used to the missionary spirituality of the under-side of society. Christians of the well-to-do mid-

---

9. Harvey Cox, *Fire from Heaven. The Rise of Pentecostal Spirituality and the Reshaping of Religion in the Twenty-First Century* (London: Cassels, 1996), p. xvii. Cox quotes the French writer Gilles Kepel.
10. Harvey Cox, *Fire from Heaven*, p. 107.
11. Richard Shaull and Waldo Cesar, *Pentecostalism and the Future of the Christian Churches: Promises, Limitations, Challenges* (Grand Rapids: Eerdmans, 2000) pp. 115 ff.

dle-classes often show themselves to be indifferent. They have conformed too much to the ways of this world and cherish the material achievements of welfare and security. Even as Christians, we are bound up with a society that in the wake of 9/11 thinks it can shut itself off from the distress and poverty of two-thirds of the world's population.

In their own country, the churches have practically no contact with people in depressed urban areas. Let alone that we should be able to understand even a little of how the poor live. What do we know of how they relate with God in the daily struggle to survive? The Pentecostal theologian C.B. Johns challenges us to no longer avoid meeting those who are excluded from modernity. It could just happen that we gain a new experience of God in such a meeting.

> Whoever goes in search of the spirituality from the under-side of society, risks a mysterious and dangerous journey to the kingdom of the Spirit, the Spirit of Christ, who prefers to be in the margins.[12]

Such a meeting can serve our own healing. Our own society shows signs of sickness that disturb us and make us uncertain. Feelings of uneasiness and insecurity take alarming forms. Having previously considered ourselves to be unassailable and superior, we are now more aware of our vulnerability. But it remains an uncomfortable thought: being offered help from, of all people, those who in our eyes had for so long depended on our pity.

HEALING COMMUNITIES IN THE BIJLMER

One does not need to travel to the South to get to know healing churches. There are plenty in our large cities. After a seemingly incurable illness, God gifted the Ghanaian Daniel Himmans Arday with healing, together with the calling to go abroad to lead lost souls back to God's vineyard, people of all colours and races.[13] Himmans now has a flourishing church in the Bijlmer suburb of Amsterdam. This has the wonderful name True Teachings of Christ's Temple. Himmans underlines: 'healing is part of the programme'. In other words, it is about more than just the healing power of a chosen medium. Healing is rather a task of the whole local congregation, which functions as a place for healing.

Physical and mental troubles receive treatment. People on whom doctors have

---

12. Cheryl Bridges Johns, 'Meeting God in the Margins: Ministry Among Modernity's Refugees'. In: *The Papers of the Henry Luce III Fellows in Theology*, vol. 3, ed. Matthew Zyniewicz (Atlanta: Scholars Press, 1998).
13. See Gerrie ter Haar, 'Tot genezing geroepen. Een Ghanese dominee in de Bijlmer'. In: *Wereld en Zending* (2001/2) pp. 35 ff.

given up, are able to resume everyday life. But also 'healing' of things such as poverty, discrimination, violence and unemployment are dealt with in very practical ways in this church. For example, the church advises on how to enter the labour market and organises programmes aimed at taking the youth off the streets. According to Himmans, the healing ministry can complement conventional medicine. That indeed seemed to be the case in the Bijlmer disaster of 1992 [in which over 40 residents, many Third-World migrants, died when a cargo plane ploughed into a couple of high-rise blocks of flats.] The religious communities in the Bijlmer played a remarkable role in the processing of the traumas at the time.

Another healing community in the same Amsterdam suburb is the House of Fellowship. The congregation, whose 90 members are mainly of African origin, is one of the 100 migrant churches that enrich the Dutch capital. The ministry of healing is mainly aimed at the comprehensive liberation of African and other foreign women who are victims of women-trafficking. The aim is to free as many black slaves in the red-light district of Amsterdam from prostitution and help them start a new existence. Marfo has so far been able to liberate about 300 women from forced prostitution by means of political acts and exorcism. An impressive example of the struggle against modern slavery in the heart of Amsterdam.[14]

Whoever gets to know The House of Fellowship, encounters a place of hope in a desolate neighbourhood. Feeling uprooted in the diaspora – in which foreigners and their rights seem to be granted ever less space and with racial tensions on the rise – men, women and children experience the liberating power of the Gospel in body and soul. In the many forms of brokenness, the church is recognised by young and old as a place for healing. Therein also lies its attraction. Spirituality and engagement, diaconal service and proclamation, personal faith and social-political action are all interconnected. Jesus is called upon as the one who forgives sins and who heals, who casts out demons and who gives people back their dignity and rights. The Spirit brings the individual to conversion and sanctification of life, but also inspires to prophetic resistance against exploitation and slavery.

The established churches still view the African and other non-Western churches with a touch of compassion, as though they are exotic relics found in the old mission collection-box; an old-time religion that the enlightened Christian has outgrown. The reality is often different and can be surprising. Despite all the (critical) questions that a visit to The House of Fellowship sparks off in Western observers, one cannot escape the conviction that this church-in-the-diaspora reflects the non-

---

14. Tom Marfo, 'Wie geboeid zijn, Hij bevrijdt ze...' In: *Wereld en Zending* (2002/4) pp. 71 ff.

Western face of the fast-growing world-church in the 21st century. A practical religion that gives coherence to a fragmented life; an expression of following Christ that substantially contributes to reconciliation between peoples and races; and a source of missionary spirituality that gives society direction and a goal to strive for.

JESUS AND THE MINISTRY OF HEALING

Bearing in mind all that has been written so far in this article, we finally turn to the Gospels. We try to read them anew – as it were, reading over the shoulder of an African, seen through their eyes and from the perspective of their culture. What are we told about Jesus' approach to illness and healing? In each of the four gospel accounts, healings have a very central place in the programme of Jesus.[15]

Just take the opening chapters of the gospel according to Matthew. In chapter 4, the evangelist tells of Jesus' first public appearances. 'From that time Jesus began to proclaim, "Repent, for the kingdom of heaven has come near".' (Mt 4.17) It is as if his mission can be written on a single fingernail, to be summed up as 'the proclamation of the good news that the kingdom of God is near at hand'. The church's mission today is nothing more and nothing less. Its primary task, wherever in the world, remains: the proclamation of the Gospel of the Kingdom.

Matthew said remarkable things about what that implies and the way in which Jesus proclaims the good news. One's attention is first drawn to where Jesus first appears in public. They who live on the edge of dark Galilee experience the fulfillment of Isaiah's prophecy: the people who walk in darkness shall see a great light. In the hills by the lake of Galilee, the invitation, the promise that is bound up with the proclamation of the good news, is received with joy: turn to Jesus and you yourself shall witness it! (Mt 3.17). By following Jesus, the people see great things happen!

It cannot have escaped our attention that in our era it is precisely in the 'Galilee areas' of our world – those at the bottom of society, on the margins of the world of the rich – where the light of the Gospel is most noticed.[16] That gives cause for

---

15. See John Christopher Thomas, 'The Spirit, healing and mission: An overview of the Biblical Canon'. In: *International Review of Mission* 93 (2004) pp. 421 ff. Also: N.A. Schuman, *Al deze woorden. Over het Evangelie naar Mattheüs* (Meinema, 1991) appreciates the well-considered composition of the first Gospel and its accounts of healing.
16. 'Third-World' theologians further develop the 'Galilee Principle' with regard to their marginalised context. See, for example, Virgilio Elizondo, *Galilean Journey. The Mexican-American Promise* (Orbis, 2002).

thought. Not in the centres of power, such as Jerusalem and Judea, but of all places in Galilee one experiences that in Jesus Christ the Kingdom is liberating and really present. But how then?

The evangelist goes on to give a detailed account of how Jesus appears in public (up to chapter 16). First he gives a summary account (Mt 4.23-25). Again it is said that Jesus proclaims the Gospel of the Kingdom. And now we hear how this proclamation takes place: Jesus 'teaches' and he 'heals'. 'Teaching' and 'healing' are the two activities that accompany the 'proclaiming'. We can recognise the Greek words: *kerussein* (preaching, proclaiming), *didaskein* (teaching) and *therapeuein* (healing, restoring). English offers us an aid by which to remember these: Jesus is *preaching,* by *teaching* and *healing* (Mt 4.23).

This holistic mission is neatly reflected in the structure of Matthew's gospel. First we hear how and what Jesus teaches. We find this brought together in the Sermon on the Mount. There, Jesus brings the Torah up to date by giving radical directions about the path of discipleship (Mt 5-7). This is followed by detailed accounts of how Jesus performs acts of healing during his travels. We become witnesses to a series of ten acts of healing, as an equal number of signals that the Kingdom is at hand (Mt 8-9). He who is teacher is at the same time wholly healer.

Here is a brief line-up: the first – also principal – sign of the Kingdom is the healing of a leper. A human being who cannot take part in society because of his illness, is the first to experience that the heavenly kingdom breaks through all boundaries. That is emphasised by the evangelist immediately linking this act of healing with the Sermon on the Mount. Jesus descends from the mount of 'teaching', followed by great crowds, 'and there was a leper who came to him and knelt before him' (Mt 8.2). Matthew thus places the mount of the Sermon on the Mount, the mount of instruction, in close proximity to a lepers' colony. The teaching about the Kingdom is given in the immediate neighbourhood of a place of misery.

Jesus then goes on to heal the servant of a Roman centurion, the mother-in-law of Peter, two demoniacs, a paralyzed man, the daughter of Jairus, a woman suffering from hemorrhages, two blind men and a mute demoniac. That is nine so far. Where then is the tenth account of an act of healing? Suddenly you discover Matthew, the tax-collector: he is one of those who are sick, of whom Jesus says that he too needs a healer (Mt 9.12). Can one not also talk of a healing miracle when someone who is addicted to money and possessions, is freed from the demon that is the love of money and learns to share with others?

So, ten healing miracles that point to the dawning of the Messianic age. That is also what Jesus indicates when he answers the question posed by the disciples of

John the Baptist, as to whether he is the one who is to come, or whether they are to wait for another. They are given to understand that they have to report to John what they hear and see: 'The blind receive their sight, the lame walk, the lepers are cleansed, the deaf hear, the dead are raised, and the poor have good news brought to them' (Mt 11.5).

The following is of great importance: in the middle of these ten healing stories, Matthew places a quotation from the well-known song of the servant of the Lord in Isaiah 53. He sees there being a close link between the healing ministry of Jesus and that of the suffering servant. In Jesus he recognises the *wounded healer*: 'He took our infirmities and bore our diseases' (Mt 8.16-17). It concerns a marvellous mystery: he who himself was beaten and wounded, is thus able to heal the weals of others. Our peace (*shalom*, wholeness) lies in the torment which he willingly underwent.

The series of healings is concluded with almost the same words with which the description of Jesus' public appearances began. Again a summary account, this time looking back (Mt 9.35-38). And again the verbs 'teaching' and 'healing' accompany the core activity – 'proclaiming'. Jesus proclaims the good news. He does this by teaching and no less by healing (Mt 9.35). The two activities cannot to be separated out. Instead, they form a holistic togetherness. The signs are explained in Jesus' teaching. Conversely, the truth of his words is underlined by the signs that he performs. What is new here is that Matthew points to the deepest motivation, the source of Jesus' public appearances. On seeing the crowds of people, lost and wandering sheep without a shepherd, he is moved to have compassion for them (Mt 9.36).

Seeing this in its entirety, there can be no other conclusion than that the ministry of healing has an unbelievably important role in Jesus' mission, as a non-verbal form of proclamation and sign of the coming Kingdom. And if that counts for the mission of Jesus, should that then not also count for the mission of his followers?

The summary account of Mt 9 concludes with the image of the harvest, which is plentiful, and the workers who are few (Mt 9.38). This lays the link with what immediately follows in Mt 10: the sending-out of the twelve apostles. They are given 'authority over unclean spirits, to cast them out, and to cure every disease and every sickness' (Mt 10.1). The disciples take part in Jesus' mission: 'As you go, proclaim the good news, 'The kingdom of heaven has come near.' Cure the sick, raise the dead, cleanse the lepers, cast out demons' (Mt 10.7-8). The aspect of 'teaching', as a form of participating in the mission of Jesus, is stressed in the great commission: 'teaching them to obey everything that I have commanded you' (Mt 28.19).

THE WOUNDED HEALER

The followers go no other way than that of the Master. The risen Lord is none other than the one who is marked by suffering and fatally wounded. He will forever remain recognisable by the scars of his suffering on his side and hands, authentic evidence that it really is him. The broken figure of Christ is the same who heals the broken world. It was precisely because he did not want to come down from the cross and save himself, that he saved others (Mt 27.42). There is a special and paradoxical character to his kingship. 'Jesus reigns from the wood.' To him who was crucified is given the authority by his Father, now that he has fulfilled his will (Mt 28.18). This all has no small consequences for the style that befits the church and its mission. The notion of following the wounded healer will preserve us from triumphalism and the striving for power. After all, God's power manifests itself in human weakness.[17]

To avoid misunderstanding, it is necessary to underline three issues concerning the public appearance of Jesus:

1. It is never just about a miraculous healing. Jesus' acts of healing move between faith and following. Miracles are pointers to the new, to that which still awaits fulfilment. Everything is directed to the final breaking-through of the Kingdom that is to come. Wherever Jesus happens to be, something of the healing power of the Kingdom always comes to light. The wholeness that Jesus gives, embraces salvation [heil] in all its liberating dimensions, for body, soul and spirit. Healing and forgiveness can therefore also not be viewed separately. It is the Saviour's [Heiland] concern to act so that the lost human being find the way back to the Father, to the neighbour and to oneself.
The lesson that the Ghanaian Pentecostal theologian Opoku Onyinah draws from Matthew's gospel – a lesson that is not just interesting for the African context – is that faith is not so much a condition for experiencing the healing power of

---

17. Henri Nouwen, in *The Wounded Healer. Ministry in Contemporary Society* (New York, 1972), has developed profound thoughts about this as regards the ministry: 'In our own woundedness, we can become a source of life for others'. See also Mercy Amba Oduyoye, 'De gewonde genezer in Afrika'. In: Manuela Kalsky, *De gewonde genezer: christologie vanuit het perspectief van vrouwen in verschillende culturen* (Baarn: Ten Have, 1991) p. 13. She relates the expression to the suffering of African women as victims (twice over) in situations of injustice and poverty. 'The Christ of which I speak is the Jesus of the Bible, not the Christ of the dogmas. The Christ is this man Jesus, who himself experienced the power of the devil. That is why he knows how to destroy [the devil's] power over others and how he can heal those who are wounded by the structures of death. Having himself been wounded, he became our "wounded healer".'

Jesus, but rather a result of that.[18] Many gain faith and find the path of disciple-ship by means of a healing experience. The fundamental orientation on the ini-tiative of Jesus keeps faith and magic apart.

2. Jesus' acts of healing are also seen in terms of the victory over the power of Satan. He healed those who had come under the devil's spell. Jesus saw the Satan falling from heaven. In his approach to the sick, Jesus breaks through prevailing explanations. And yet, in certain situations, sickness and being possessed really are associated with the world of demons and evil spirits. It is worth studying the relevant Bible passages again, reading over the shoulder of African Christians. How can exorcism get a well-considered place in pastoral care?

3. The social aspect of the acts of healing is important. Medical recovery is but one aspect of the whole matter. Illnesses such as leprosy, epilepsy, blood-loss and so on, cause people to be treated as pariahs and outcasts. Jesus seeks out those who are rejected and touches unclean people. He gives them back their place in the community. He deliberately breaks with taboos and through barriers that divide people and groups. He challenges the established order by healing on, of all days, the Sabbath.

CONCLUSION

It is a fact that Jesus' healing ministry is much closer to the daily life of non-Western Christians than to us as children of the Enlightenment. In Western soci-ety it is clear: medicine is practised in the hospital, religion in the church. But in Africa and Latin America, healing is an integral part of the church's ministry. This should not astonish us. There where people have no access to health care, only one path remains – the path that leads to above. And that seems to be open: countless people gain faith by way of healing. One not just hears the biblical accounts of Jesus who heals the sick and casts out demons. One also knows them to be part of one's own experience. Many physically experience what Jesus taught about a God of mercy, who binds up wounds and becomes a source of life amid death and brings joy amid suffering.

Whenever we seek contemporary forms of healing ministry, we have to keep our ears open for the experiences of God by those who are vulnerable and who suf-fer, both in the global South and in the North. It is by being in practical solidar-ity with them that we become aware of the presence and the actions of the Spirit of the Saviour ('healer'); and thus we gain ears with which to hear what the Spirit

---

18. Opoku Onyinah, 'Matthew Speaks to Ghanaian Healing Situations'. In: *Journal of Pentecostal Theology* 10/1 (October, 2001) p. 133.

says to today's congregation. The Pentecostal theologian Steven J. Land (Cleveland) eloquently expresses this insight from his perspective:

> With regard to missionary praxis, perhaps a fruitful, specific place to start would be a shared healing ministry. In prayer for and ministry to the sick, oppressed, demonized and suffering, Pentecostals could participate with other Christians in a missionary praxis which could be at once a sign of the last days' ministry, a gift of the Holy Spirit, a sacrament symbolizing the mystery of the wounded healer, and an expression of the most central and most needed of the affections for the time between the times, compassion.[19]

As fruit of this praxis, a new paradigm for Christian witness and service for the 21st century could be discovered, leaving behind the old patterns and institutional separations of 'ecumenism', 'mission', 'evangelism', 'diakonia', 'pastoral care' and 'liturgy', in favor of an integral approach of healing ministry in the footsteps of Jesus. The mission of the church nowadays is, amid the brokenness and in conflict situations, to offer 'healing places' where men, women and children find 'healing' for body, mind and soul; welcoming meeting-places where wholeness, reconciliation and forgiveness are received and shared.

---

19. Steven J. Land, *Pentecostal Spirituality. A Passion for the Kingdom* (Sheffield: Sheffield Academic Press, 1993) p. 218.

12. God in the Margins: Reflections on the Wounded Healer

Richard Shaull

During my visit to Europe, I am encouraged to discover that ecumenical and missionary movements are turning their attention to the theme of ministry of healing and communities of healing. What I want to do is present a few brief reflections on the wounded healer from the perspective of my involvement in Brazil in recent years.[1] If ever the world desperately needed women and men on fire with the power of God, committed to the struggle of restoration, it is now. At stake is the survival of hundreds of millions of impoverished people, the recreation of conditions for human existence in community and the salvation of our planet from ecological disaster.

THE WORLD OF THE POOR

The harsh reality is that, as we enter a new millennium, vast masses of women, men and children around the world are caught up in a desperate daily struggle for survival. They live in total insecurity on the periphery of our enormous cities, without any of the most basic structures of community or society, exposed every day to illness, poverty, violence and early death. They have no positive identity, no place in society. Moreover, those who live in this situation have no way of making any sense of what is happening to them, no possibility of escaping from it. They can only assume that their personal lives and their world are in the hands of supernatural demonic powers. They experience their lives and their world as *possessed*. And if they have any hope, it can only rest in a supernatural power, thus their search today becomes more religious than political.

Now, I suspect that most of us have been somewhat aware of this reality, but looked at it as rather distant from us, the hard human situation of others. I became

---

1. This article is the slightly revised text of a lecture, held by Richard Shaull during his last visit to Europe, some months before his passing away in 2003. Shaull was responding to the report *Followers of the Wounded Healer* of the Netherlands Missionary Council (NZR), written by its general secretary, Wout van Laar. The adapted text of this report is the preceding article in this book.

acutely aware of this situation during my research in Brazil and presented it in a book, which I wrote together with the Brazilian sociologist Waldo Cesar, entitled *Pentecostalism and the Future of the Christian Churches*.[2] In this publication we tried to show how we as a church might respond to their cry, with a compelling evangelical message of life and of hope. It meant that we, from our own situation of relative stability, were called to reach out in mission to them, the poor.

September 11 and subsequent events have changed that for me. Suddenly, this world we have ignored or kept at a distance, has come very near to us; we are inextricably connected with their fate. All around us are signs of this world breaking into ours. And now, a few secular writers are beginning to call our attention to this as a major threat to the future of all of us, against which we must defend ourselves.

It is not surprising that one of the most vocal of these in North America is Robert Kaplan, one of the editors of the *Atlantic Monthly* who, five or six years earlier, took a year to travel to what he called, *The Ends of the Earth*. What he saw everywhere was 'poverty, the collapse of cities, porous borders, cultural and racial strife, growing economic disparities, weakening nation-states'.[3] For him, it all added up to *anarchy*. An advancing process of social disintegration in which, in his words, 'We are not in control'. Now, after September 11, he is doing everything he can to warn us that the horrendous future he perceived earlier is already becoming a reality. In the face of it, we in Western Europe and North America need to do everything we can to preserve the great achievements of our superior Western civilization. But I think that most of us here realize that, if we in the West, from our positions of wealth and power, undertake to preserve and defend what we have at the expense of the rest of the world, this may well lead, as one of my Brazilian colleagues has put it, to a downward spiral of violence leading to a new age of barbarism.

COMMUNITIES OF HEALING

Within the Christian community, especially in mission circles, we have had a growing awareness of something else that the prophets of doom cannot see: in the very places around the world where the poverty and suffering are the great-

---

2. Richard Shaull and Waldo Cesar, *Pentecostalism and the Future of the Christian Churches*, (Grand Rapids, MI: Eerdmans, 2000)
3. Robert D. Kaplan, *The Ends of the Earth: A Journey at the Dawn of the 21st Century* (New York: Random House, 1996)

est, where marginal and excluded people are totally insecure, we witness also an unexpected explosion of faith and with it new life in community.

Four decades ago, in Latin America, we perceived the situation in which we were living as that of injustice and exploitation; the struggle of the poor as the struggle for liberation. And as we re-read our Bibles in that situation, Liberation Theology was born. Our eyes were opened to the presence of a compassionate God present in the lives and struggles of the poor for their liberation. We came to know Jesus of Nazareth as the one who identified himself with the poor and marginal, and who announced to them the coming of God's Reign, a new order of peace and justice. And as the poor experienced the presence and power of this God in their midst, they became part of a community of struggle which offered them security and hope.

Today, however, the masses of poor people are living a different reality. And in that situation, they are also finding a response of faith emerging as they are re-reading their Bibles. They find that God speaks a Saving Work directly to them. One compelling way of naming their situation is that proposed in the previous article: The marginal people of the world today face a situation of brokenness. They are broken women and men, living in a broken society. But in the midst of it, they experience, beyond the dire reality and predictions of Kaplan and others, a Presence and Power which brings healing and creates community in the midst of the violence around them. They are rediscovering the Jesus who enters into their brokenness, and gives his life in a ministry of healing, the healing of the full human being in a community of healing.

By centering on this theme, I believe, we are called to situate ourselves on one of the major frontiers of the movement of the Spirit at this time.

We are challenged to re-examine, perhaps re-create, our missionary witness around something we and our churches have largely ignored until now, the central place of healing in both the life and witness of Jesus. For example, in the first chapters of the Gospel of Matthew, *Jesus proclaims the Good News through teaching and healing*. In fact, it is through the healing that people see what the Good News is and are drawn to Jesus. Anointed with the power of the Spirit over demonic forces, he not only proceeded to heal the sick, raise the dead, cleanse lepers and drive out demons, signs that God's Kingdom is already present in power. *He commissioned his disciples to do the same things.*

As someone committed over a lifetime to the task of theological reflection on the mission of the church, I believe that, as we concentrate our focus on the ministry of healing in a broken world, we will be able to build – on the foundation laid by liberation theology – something as significant for the next decades as was the theological work undertaken by Latin American theologians earlier.

If and when we do this, we are forced to face one disturbing fact for us members of mission societies. While we, over a long period of time, have seen ourselves as those who are the bearers of a healing ministry to the peoples of other lands, the stark reality is that this dynamic message of the healing of broken people and a broken world is evident primarily among religious movements in the South – in Latin America, Africa and some parts of Asia – not in the West. Not in the churches rooted in the Reformation of the 16th century, but in movements loosely defined as Charismatic and Pentecostal.

As I have entered into this world of broken people, I have seen this power for healing, which we see in Jesus, present especially in Pentecostal circles. And how this takes place is not difficult to see. Women and men find that they can enter into the Realm of the Spirit and there find themselves embraced by, filled with the Divine Spirit. Through a profoundly moving, often ecstatic experience, their broken chaotic lives are reconstructed. Men and women whose entire being is riddled with disease, experience healing. Those who have no sense of self-worth, discover – as one young Pentecostal woman put it – that they are jewels in the eyes of God. Those, whose lives had fallen apart and were powerless to do anything about it, find themselves called and empowered to create a new future for themselves. And, most amazing of all, those who are most broken, find in this experience a basis for security in the midst of violence and total insecurity. As they are healed, they become a community of healing whose members penetrate into the world around them. In a world where there is no hope, they find themselves grounded in an experience of new life which calls them toward the future. In fact, their experience of healing and of being a healing community as a result of the Presence of the Spirit is such that from that point onward, they are involved in creating the future.

Let me sight only one example. The immense *favelas* of Rio de Janeiro are centres of the most incredible violence, as drug dealers and police battle each other constantly. Each new generation grows up in the *favelas* in anonymity and powerlessness. The drug dealers and gang leaders offer these young men the one possibility they can see of breaking out of this closed world. But if and when these young men discover what they have gotten into by joining one of these gangs and want to break away, they can't. They will be killed – unless they can prove to those who control them that they have been converted in one of the little Pentecostal churches in the *favela* and are following that path. Many of these little churches have become a safe, violence-free zone; they are communities of healing in the midst of all the destruction and death around them.

All of this is happening now. I have seen it. I have experienced healing through them and have been changed by contact with them. I have found here an experience which could offer healing to us in the West in our manifold conditions of brokenness. At the same time, this authentic biblical healing ministry is time and again threatened by superficial knowledge of the faith, by the temptations of power which corrupts, by easy appeals to the weakness of women and men rather than proclaiming and living the depths of faith, by the temptation to use the Bible for their own ends rather than submitting themselves constantly to the Word. But given our absence from that world, we should be slow to rush to judgment.

RE-SITUATION AMONG THE POOR

If we take all this seriously, we cannot escape the fact that it calls for a radical change in our mission strategy: a decision first of all to enter into the world of the poor, to re-situate ourselves among the poor. Now, this doesn't just mean re-situating ourselves geographically among the poor, although that in itself would mean a formidable change of direction. To enter the world of the poor means to enter into their *religious* world, and allow ourselves to become broken by that experience and thus become wounded healers as Christ was.

And it means something much more difficult: Even when we do situate ourselves among the poor, as we have done from time to time, our mission schools and our churches have tended to move each new generation farther and farther from the poor. Participation in the church becomes a process of formation to become middle-class professionals.

Presbyterians began work in Brazil in 1859 and the church has grown considerably, moving gradually away from the poorest. Among the vast majority of poor people, the Pentecostals have had astonishing growth. But when recently a seminary student in Rio asked the President of the *Igreja Presbiteriana do Brazil* (Presbyterian Church of Brazil) what this historic church was doing among the poor, his immediate response was: 'We are a middle-class church'. And he recognised fairly: we who prepared a new generation of pastors and lay leaders, did not prepare them to take the one step necessary – to situate the church among the poor.

Our traditional churches usually are not going to take these steps toward solidarity with the poor. But there is one thing we can do – and that is urgently needed. We can find ways of relating authentically to Christian communities, largely Pentecostal, who are living this relationship. That can only become true, if we are willing to become wounded – to go through a process of *kenosis* which permits us to relate to them and engage in dialogue with them, on their terms, not ours. That in itself is something we have hardly begun to do.

A second radical change is called for: not just to move toward the world of the poor but also *to be open to their witness to us* – and this with a very specific focus. Because of their tremendous experience of the Spirit, they can live in hope and with security in an insecure and violent world. Through this experience, they can help us to live the same way, as the chaotic world around us moves more and more – not toward liberation but toward greater chaos, violence and barbarism. This is the gift we can receive from them.

But here again, we will have to pay a high price to receive this gift. We are called, I contend, to wager that the Holy Spirit is doing 'a new thing' among these communities of healing among those who are most broken. And if that is the case, our relationship with them must be one in which we allow the Spirit to address us through them. In other words, we who earlier were the bearers of a message which called upon others to be transformed, now face the possibility that those who received and responded to that message present us with the challenge to be transformed. That cannot happen as long as we remain safely enclosed within our religious world and look on these dynamic Pentecostal movements as *peculiar*, to use the word of one Presbyterian leader in Brazil. We can only be transformed when we get to the point where we expect that the Spirit – which is not only moving in their midst but through them – is addressing us as well.

TOWARDS A NEW PARADIGM

Moreover, I am convinced that we must take one step more. For what captivated me in the midst of our research was the possibility that Pentecostals have this dynamic and contagious faith, and are able to bring about healing and become communities of healing because *they have arrived at a different understanding of their faith – what I would call a new theological paradigm.*

It is true that also we in the West need a new paradigm, a new pattern of relationships and of service. 'A new paradigm for Christian witness and service for the 21st century could be discovered, leaving behind the old patterns and institutional separations of "ecumenism", "mission", "evangelism", "diakonia", "pastoral care" and "liturgy", in favour of an integral approach of healing ministry in the footsteps of Jesus.'[4]

Here is not the place or time to explore this. But it could just be that what they are striving to articulate and live, with all its limitations, is precisely an understanding and experience of the Christian faith which moves beyond where we are.

---

4. Wout van Laar, *Churches as Healing Communities*, p. 145 in this book.

And it may be this which prepares them to live in the midst of almost total insecurity and live toward the future.

The test of Christian faith will be its ability to provide resources for finding meaning and direction in a time when the old order is collapsing and the shape of a new future is hidden. Jesus of Nazareth lived in such a time. His life centered in the experience and power of a compassionate God in the world, providing those around him with an alternative vision of reality and community. Today, as the resurrected Christ continues to be active in our midst through the Spirit, we have these same resources at our disposal. Whether we make use of this transforming power is a question that we have not yet answered.

13. Healing Power in the True Teachings of Christ's Temple. A Personal Witness

Daniel Himmans-Arday

I am humbled and greatly honoured by the invitation to share my insight and experience with you.

Is there anything called supernatural healing? Is there a possibility that a 'miraculous' healing can occur? Yes sir, there is. And I am a 'walking' testimony to it. Don't take my word for it, but just hear me out and then draw your own conclusion.

Miraculous healing through an invincible energy or power we Christians call 'Almighty God', does not depend solely on my personal encounter with or experience of Him, but also on a wider range of observations that I made, plus the proven facts that there is an invincible hand at work in all of us. The birth of one, the growth of one and the inventive intelligence of one can never be safely attributed solely to that folded 'hemispheric' cushion on top of our heads, called 'brain'. There is certainly a propelling 'POWER' beyond that composition. Observing the 'unaided' healing of a swollen hand, a wound closing up, a joining of broken bones; and the thrilling sensation on finger-tips and eye-lids – they all tell me that we are 'blessed' with a receiving 'dish' inside everyone of us. And when we are ready to receive instructions from the Creator of our being, this will be a real source of healing for all creation indeed (see 2 Chron 7.14).

By the implications of the above quotation, we can deduce that the act of healing covers a far wider field than can be imagined. Here we can convincingly say that any obstacle that impairs a human's free movement can be termed as sickness needing a cure. Some ailments can be self-inflicted and others can be human injustice to fellow humans. The very earth that we walk upon is sick and needing redemption (see Rom 8.22). If we accept this, then our careful treatment of things will also bring healing to the very nature on which our lives depend upon. For a good soil produces good harvest to feed us, because hunger is also a sickness! Self-inflicted ailments are the self-abused ones (such as excessive smoking, drinking, sleepless nights) and human injustices being dealers (of drugs) that disregard the suffering of people they sell to.

To cover all this in my address will be stretching the matter too far. But all the same, the truth of the matter is that there is a 'POWER' that heals. And since new awareness of this has come to light, it is only proper that we, the believers, investigate thoroughly and in the process be convinced of its existence. Never before has the pursuit of health absorbed so many people so much of the time than this present period of our life. Just switch on the television and confirm the following: Swedish and Norwegian diet programme; awareness and warning of spread of Aids; British health warning of dangers of obesity; bird flu epidemic warnings by the World Health Organisation; and so on.

Because of this, all those treatments have come under growing scrutiny more than ever. Some have praised medicine's strides to combat and control ailments. Others have criticised it for its slow pace to catch up with the times and, as such, have branched out into the alternatives. More about that later. For the Christian, the realisation that we are not alone and need Godly help and acceptance of its existence to enable all of us – more especially the gifted and anointed ones – to use this phenomenon, is very important. Many of us Christians have relegated the process of healing (as Jesus healed; see Mt 15.31-37) to the distant memories. And the concept of treating the body as a whole (mind, spirit and body) seems to have been limited to the basic premises of only those who deal with therapeutic energies. Holistic medicine which is based on treating this mind-spirit-body and the unifying factor being always energy, does not apply to many anymore. (Note: 'holistic' originated from the Greek word 'holos'.)

I believe that while the doctor treats us as 'organs' needing five or more 'experts' all touching on our different organs within us, it is only natural that we are treated as whole, full and complete individuals. And this can come about only through Godly-revealed ways when medicine is failing. There is no doubt in my mind that in this our modern time, the new technological know-how is driving many, many intelligent people – as well as people of good will – to agree that a new consciousness has been born. And this new awareness permeates every aspect of our culture, from lifestyle to medicine. A lifestyle that would have been frowned upon even 20 years ago, is now being received and accepted with all the challenges that it possesses unto the human race – with gleeful satisfaction even among the faith of the Christians.

The human health, long neglected by social norms – like smoking cigarettes, alcohol, careless sex, cutting of virgin's skins (in Africa) – is now being noticed, protected, cared for and sought after by so many people so much of the time. Medicine, with its ever progressing successes in surgical techniques, is being praised and queried at the same time by society.

The dissatisfied ones have sought cures in alternative medicines such as acupuncture, herbal cure, applications of unscientifically tested medications (some of which the church refers to as occult practices), yogas and others. All these efforts can be unnecessary if mankind has fixed its sight on the Creator of all things, who is the prime giver of all healing energy. Listen to Him again: 'If my people who are called by my name [meaning us Christians] will humble themselves and pray, and seek my face and turn from their wicked ways, THEN will I hear them from heaven and will FORGIVE their sins and WILL heal their land' (2 Chron 7.14).

This is my conviction, brethren: in this world, nature itself tells us that there are 'sanctified' people who talk for the folks. And that's why we have presidents, police chiefs, pilots, captains, spokesmen, women, priests, and so on. In this life, as far as goodness is concerned, the Christian faith's spokesorgans are the sanctified institutions which are known as the church and whose doctrine is the healing of the soul. Humility is the mother of peace, for it seeks no more than its own fair share of joy. Prayer is the food of the soul by which good thoughts can ALWAYS permeate our environments. Repentance is to stop hurting each other. Seeking His face means studying His words and skilful living (Mt 10.16). Piling up 'arsenals' to defend one's self is not the way forward, but harmonious living is. And that is fully established repentance.

When all these are met, the 'higher hands' above can be reached and our healing guaranteed. And from the crying earth to the perplexed and ailing body, we shall be there. While the doctors heal by means of observing symptoms, the Christian church applies the preventive method. That is called PRAYER. And here is the modern Christian problem. In this modem days of advanced technology; where verification is no longer an optional but a 'must'; in which many of us are still grasping for answers to the causes of the sudden appearances of unexplained ailments, despite our excessive prayers, which the Bible guarantees us is the only source of preventing decay, ailments and suffering; one cannot just wake up and tell another: 'There is a spiritual energy in my hands; for I have been called with power to bless you or heal you, so come to my God for your healing if the doctors have failed' or 'I have seen the LIGHT, so follow me'.

Knowing 'something' is one thing. Proving that 'something' is totally a different ball-game altogether. But then remembering the difficulties of our ancient fathers of the faith in proving what was the truth, I am greatly encouraged by my belief that one day all mankind will come to know that there is an Almighty God who has planted his 'healing' energy in us all and, as such, we only need to direct that 'dish' called 'hearts in us' towards Him and – presto! – we are restored.

After all, when Galileo tried to explain that gravity was a 'universal force' that enables the earth – which is round – to go around the sun, he was imprisoned. Years and years after his death, the world came to know the truth. So also shall many of us be persecuted for knowing what we now know. In chapter 10 of my latest book, titled *And the Truth shall set you free*, when I revealed of the spiritual power that becomes identical to the Holy Spirit of the mighty prophets of yesterday, I was mistaken to be preaching reincarnation when that was not my goal at all.

The power of Christian prayers is like a ring – it has no end. The praying congregation prays and when things happen to be beyond them, I approach the Elders for anointing (see Mk 6.13; Jas 5.7-20). When things are beyond them, the Elders approach the Head Elder who is 'sanctified' for further strengthening (see Lk 22.31). And the 'anointed' – because he or she is always being tested by forces and strengthened by the Almighty ALWAYS, irrespective of his or her current condition – reminds the congregation to continue praying for him (see, for example, 1 Thess 5.25). They usually do this to help him avoid the pitfalls of this life, if it is possible (see Acts 12.12-14).

But, brethren, it's not only the world of doubters who question the authority of the Christian healing process. Some Christians even find it hard to understand certain things as well, more especially when their prayers (and revealed methods as Jesus; see John 11) seem to be producing nothing but more miseries as well. Many fail to know that there are still mysteries surrounding man and that it's only a matter of patience that we need to overcome those troubling times!

Friends, remember: patience always wins. Agreeing that whatever conditions we are in today, we are still sick and needing His healing grace. We must pray regularly to prevent our rapid demise. The word of God has made room for us to tackle those parasites, should they ever become a bother to us. And that is where the truly anointed ones come in. They might not possess all the answers but, believe me, their presence ignites real fire that heals the body!

My own experience started a very long time ago when still in my 20s (I am an old man now). I was a very good footballer, an educated junior officer in the army, an assistant chief compositor of the Armed Forces Printing Press and a soccer captain of the Defence Force Football Team, a somewhat loose Christian and by birth a Methodist Christian. On that day, after a training session, I went to a friend's house to take my shower and dress for work. As an officer in higher places, I needed to be at work everyday. So, instead of going home, which was very far away from the training field, it was only proper that I bathe in a friend's house.

As I went under the shower, I felt a very heavy 'hand' pull me down towards the ground. I was choking and becoming breathless. I wanted to scream, but found that I had lost my voice. But then suddenly, 'an unseen hand' – whose fingers I felt but saw no-one – pulled and pushed me outside in my nakedness unto the compound of the house. And that was it!

When I came to, I was at the General Hospital (of the military). And this place was to be a home to me on and off for the following three years. I was on three occasions written off and on each occasion revived. One day, when all hope of me ever recovering was given up, while still awake in a very deep night hour, I heard a noise. I opened my eyes (widely). I saw the ceiling of my room go off and then the sky pierce through the roof. A basket appeared, full of people robely dressed (of which, I was told, represented the disciples). In their midst, a sparklingly robed voice whispered a message: 'Daniel, you are healed today, and you will win new souls for me in a distant land. Be guided by my Spirit' (Mt 10.10).

Then suddenly everything became still. Everything was back to normal. But then I felt a heavy power of energy pierce through my body, and then I woke – surprised but healed. My wife was 'lamentably' sleeping in the room next to mine, and when she saw me standing beside her, she nearly fainted. She thought she was seeing a ghost. And when I requested that we pray together, she was speechless. You see, we have never prayed together before in all our years of marriage and better words I have never prayed alone before, besides the collective ones we did during church service.

From that day suddenly I was giving messages and predictions – which were all accurate and I still do that – and then greater understanding to scriptures were opened to me – something that I never possessed before. Whenever I pray, answers are got, and there were other things that I was inspired to do, as well as the person I have become. I saw my own lifestyle changed before me and suddenly realised, with a new looking back on all these events before this episode, that I encountered several mysterious 'coincidences' that have now come to make me know that the Almighty God was preparing me for his service long before I was born.

A few examples of such 'coincidences' being: at eight I nearly got drowned in a big river. At nine I told my dad while strolling with him along the beach that there will be a fish in his hat. Hours later there was and a year later he was dead. A huge bus was reversing when it stopped just short of where I had fallen down. I got up and went to thank the driver for saving my life, but the bus driver replied: 'Thanking me for what? I was not knowing that anyone was lying down behind

the bus. My damn brakes just jammed and stopped. Damn these modern brakes.'
And so on.

In my first book, *Light on the Scriptures*, I wrote a little about myself. Because
this book was privately published, I have reserved it on compact disc for any
publisher with interest to produce it on the wider market. A few copies are with
my church secretary, B.B. Botchey. My second book, of which I wrote at length
about myself, can be obtained at bookshops in Amsterdam, and also at Foyles
Bookshop in London. This latest book, *And the Truth shall set you free*, also gives
some exciting revelations about the life of the African Christian.

A PROSPECTIVE EPILOGUE – The Power of the Spirit and the Spirit of Power

André Droogers

An epilogue offers an opportunity to look back at contributions and themes in a personal way. At the margin of the book, a closing statement is made, literally as an epi-phenomenon to what is central to this collection of articles. However, an epilogue is not only written for retrospection. Prospecting the future is an inevitable challenge – including adventure and risk – to the author of such a text.

I will not try to summarize this book, nor will I refer explicitly to the preceding articles, although the other authors have certainly put me on a track for my own reflection. I will consider the three themes around which this book is organized – pluralism, dialogue and healing – in their connectedness, at least as I would construct it from my subjective standpoint, as a cultural anthropologist of religion with a scholarly interest in Pentecostalism but also as a member of a mainline church. From my own idiosyncratic frame of reference, I will look at the themes that are discussed in this book.

My leitmotiv will be the reciprocal relationship between power and meaning. I use power in the classical sociological sense as the more or less exclusive capacity to influence a person's or a group's behavior, even against their will, using the reserved access to resources as a basis for the application of this capacity. Meaning is the result of the application of another human capacity, generally available, to make sense, in a more or less systematic way, of reality and of experiences with that reality. In my view, power and meaning are prominent elements in religions, even though believers prefer to reserve the word 'power' for the sacred and tend to avoid it when referring to human beings and their behavior. The two concepts should be considered in their interaction and dialectics. Power depends on the meaning that legitimates those in power (for example, called by God), whereas meaning will be selectively constructed within the parameters that power relations dictate (such as through church discipline).

Viewed in this way, power and meaning will be shown to be central to such themes as pluralism, dialogue and healing. The Power of the Spirit cannot be understood without discussing the Spirit of Power. In the following sections, I will explore this approach, summarily discussing each of the three themes. In closing this epilogue, power and meaning will be reconsidered in their relevance to the understanding of Pentecostalism and especially its migrant version, including the prospects for the future.

PLURALISM

Migrant churches have added to the already impressive diversity of Pentecostal churches and movements. The first cause of this variety that an anthropologist can think of is cultural diversity. Though a world religion such as Christianity brings a universal claim with it, local expressions are inevitably influenced by the surrounding culture, even when this culture is opposed as pagan or heathen. Local churches are therefore very diverse in the concrete form they give to this faith. This is nothing new. From the start, this enculturation process was present in all the phases of Christianity's movement through the world, including its inception as the movement around Jesus of Nazareth, through its Greek, Roman and various European stages, up to its establishment in many other parts of the world. Everywhere, culture put its mark on the understanding of universal Christianity, just as nowadays the almost universal English language is always spoken with a local accent, even in Oxford.

To this cultural diversity should be added the theological and ecclesiological differences, although theology and ecclesiology themselves do not escape local cultural influences. There is always a hermeneutical problem to any understanding of the Christian message, including its expression in systematic theology and its truth claims. Moreover, besides the cultural and intellectual-academic dimensions, there is an experiential dimension, certainly so if the Spirit's charismata are part of that way of experiencing the sacred.

In short, the way in which meanings are selected from the huge reservoir of possibilities is influenced by the meanings that are prominent in the cultural context, by the demands and logic of theological reasoning and method, by church history, and by the differences in the appreciation of religious experiences. Thus every culture, academia and practice, by itself and through mutual influencing, contributes to Christian pluralism.

In the present-day age, there is an extra dimension to the cultural branding of Christianity, since cultural influences are not only felt in a local context but also through intercultural contact and communication. Missionary activities are almost by definition transcultural. The current globalizing world, in which humanity is living the experience of sharing a single space, offers many new opportunities for intercultural contact, through the mass media but also because modern, rapid means of travel are now available to many people.

Migration has become an integral part of the globalization process, affecting millions of people, with or against their will. The migrant is often pushed and pulled by power processes of an economic, ethnic and political nature. Migration is a way of giving meaning to a changed reality by moving to another place, from rural areas to the city, from a poor and unsafe country to a rich and safe country, but also sometimes from a legal to an illegal status. In migrating, people bring their religion with them. The migration process itself comes with hardships that may reinforce the migrant's need for a religious home.

Migrant churches, whether Pentecostal or not, offer such a home. They address the person's new and often precarious situation, providing not only spiritual but also material help. They serve as moral points of reference in the new situation with all its options and opportunities. To illegal migrants, they may offer an alternative status, accepting those who are refused by the officials of the host country and even offering alternative strategies, such as to marry without the state's consent but with the blessing of the church. In addition, they often bring some form of continuity with the pre-migration setting, despite the ruptures and changes that are part of the migrant's experience. They offer a new extended family, a form of artificial kinship of new brothers and sisters. The fact that they serve this function only partly explains their success. In other words: they not only help the migrant in finding his or her way through the new power game with its new rules, as played out in the new country. They also offer meaning to the new reality – a specific message that characterizes a particular church as unique. Such a church is more than an instant problem-solver, not least because people stay on after the problem is solved. They represent a world-view. Each church, despite serving the same function, will therefore have its own niche in the religious market.

Migrants use and reinterpret the many layers of meaning that the Christian message contains. Meanings are creatively and strategically reproduced as well as reproduced and updated, to make sense of the new situation. Thus, the exodus of the people of Israel may suddenly be recognized as identical to the migrant's basic experience on his or her way to the Promised Land. On the other hand, the promised land of milk and honey may not be very receptive to the newcomer, and then – instead of exodus – exile is a more appropriate biblical model, especially if the new country resembles Sodom and Gomorrah – another biblical model. Satan will be discovered to play different tricks in the new society, just as the Spirit may move in new mysterious ways.

In the new countries, through the migrant churches, the Christian message, often in its Pentecostal version, has come full circle, coming home in a situation that is quite different from the one that prevailed when the missionaries left their country as migrants of their time. In what once was the power centre of the Christian religion, migrant churches must now seek to survive in a profane plural society, where the Christian institutions no longer dominate public life and where the fact of being a Christian group no longer brings privileges. As has often been observed: to Christian migrants, the secular – to them, sinful – climate of West European societies, in particular, is an enormous disappointment. Moreover, the migrant's expectation to encounter brothers and sisters in the Spirit is not always met. The divisions in secular society between the 'autochthonous' (native) population and the migrants – representing many ethnic identities, at least as many as there once were colonies – is reflected in the contacts between Christians of the various migrant and local established churches, notwithstanding some efforts to go beyond the established boundaries. The ways to deal with power and to attribute meaning, as prevailing in the new country, often make for a climate of living apart together. The unity of Christians is frustrated by the pluralism that predominates. In that context dialogue seems indicated.

DIALOGUE

Despite all the good intentions of the participants and their willingness to listen *tabula rasa* to each other, the encounter in dialogue may also include references to power. First of all, the dialogue may include references to the power of the sacred, as when in prayer the blessing of the Lord or the Spirit's presence is asked for, apparently in the supposition that this experience will influence and change the behavior of the persons in dialogue. But the participants may also seek to influence each other's behavior and produce some change in it. Both types of influence match the definition of power as given above.

Historically grown differences may include a supposed variation in power. Pentecostal churches may therefore be thought to have a different position in comparison to so-called mainline or mainstream churches – the 'main' pointing to a dominant position. Ironically, in many countries, especially in the Southern Hemisphere, the growth of Pentecostal churches may have reversed this position, reducing the historical or missionary churches to minority status, even though they continue being labeled 'mainline'. In view of the numbers, modesty would become the mainline partners when they engage in dialogue.

To these differences, other asymmetrical types of relations can be added, in which the normal is often identified with the mainline, while the opposite is often implicitly considered deviant. An example of this is what in one of the contributions to this book is called the 'committee culture'. One may also think of a situation in which, without much discussion, the customs of academic theological debate are adopted, sometimes implicitly introducing the idea that Pentecostalism is intellectually and theologically underdeveloped or in need of help. Labels such as 'fundamentalist' and 'escapist' may in the same context be attributed to Pentecostalism. The long-standing church/sect typology has also left traces, implying that any sect is the deviation when compared with the 'normal' church. Though these presuppositions are usually made explicit and thereby criticized by dialogue representatives of these mainline churches, they may still be part of the context for dialogue, discouraging it and putting mainline participants in an awkward position with regard to their own flock. I do not mean to say that presuppositions are lacking on the Pentecostal side, but in terms of power their presumptions usually cannot be compared to those that may prevail in the mainline setting. The exception is, of course, the appeal to the power of the Spirit and the experiences that accompany this. As a consequence of these asymmetrical relationships, it is crucial that the images that are reciprocally constructed of the partners in dialogue are made explicit.

Although the dialogue with migrant Pentecostal churches often still has to be started or is in the initial stages, the set of presuppositions that reinforce the asymmetrical positions is present there as well. Moreover, migrants, generally speaking, have to deal with other setbacks. These have to do with cultural differences, but also with their status as newcomers. In some cases, newcomers are considered outsiders. They often occupy the marginal positions in society with regard to work, housing, income, education and so on. Ethnicity is another factor, which appeals to latent or even manifest feelings of racism in society.

Interestingly, an inversion may be brought about by the pride and self-consciousness of Pentecostal migrants. The idea of having preserved abroad what the native West European Christians have lost, contributes to these feelings. Moreover, the idea of a reversed mission may nourish this attitude. If the established churches fail to criticize the negative sides of secularized, modernized society, the Christians from abroad are ready to do so. The supposedly weak party thereby presents itself as the stronger party. If elements such as hospitality, community life and church participation are added to the scale, the migrant churches have more to offer than the mainline churches – and perhaps also more than the 'autochthonous' Pentecostal churches, even though the latter will share in some aspects of the inversion mentioned, especially the experience of the Spirit.

There is one aspect of the dialogue that must be mentioned here, because in a different way it has to do with power relations and the meaning-making processes that accompany them, including the self-images and the images that the partner in dialogue is labeled with. A pitfall that may frustrate dialogue occurs when there is a tendency among mainline representatives to romanticize their migrant partners in dialogue, viewing them as the noble Christians who have been able to preserve the purity that Western Christians have sacrificed to modernity and its many seductions. In linking up with the reversed mission approach, allies are supposed to be found among the non-Western migrant Christians, critical of modernity. They are thought not to be what Westerners unfortunately have become. The non-Westerner, as the term reveals, is thus defined by exclusive reference to the Westerner, not primarily by what he or she is or represents. A similar attitude can sometimes be observed when migrant Christians are invited to a mainline church service. There may be echoes here of the idea of the 'noble savage', once popular in West European philosophy, and rather resilient in popular wisdom. Such a position may be accompanied by a form of essentialist labeling, generalizing for all the non-Western cultures, as if these still have not fallen victim to modernity, let alone post-modernity. Though seemingly putting the other party in a favorable and even dominant position, the image thus constructed does not reflect the fact that all the parties involved, including the migrants, are living in a globalizing world that erodes the distinction of Western versus non-Western. The simple fact that migrants have come to West Europe and are confessing Christians is already proof of this. Nowadays nobody escapes modernity.

The sometimes idealized Afro-American origin of Pentecostalism must be viewed in the same light. The African cultures that the migrant slaves, who were involuntarily brought to the other side of the Atlantic, took with them to the New World, changed in the process and have been influenced by the dominant cultural context there – as Afro-Americans experience when they visit Africa, despite the recognition of common roots and elements. When Pentecostalism came to Africa, the cultural process was much more complex than a simple return of an African way of being religious. Dialogue would not be served by such a preconceived image of the African migrant partner.

One other variation must be mentioned in this context. Western partners in dialogue may be looking among Christian migrants for sympathetic allies in their effort to save Western culture, deemed superior because Christian, despite the fact that the same culture is one of the sources of modernity. This position can be encountered more frequently after 9/11 and the consequent identification of terrorism with Islam. The former ideological split between capitalism and communism has been replaced by a split between two world religions, despite their common roots. Such views have been developed especially in neo-conservative circles in the United States and increasingly in Europe. The media have spread a popularized version of the same message. The question is, of course, whether this view does justice to Islam. Besides, the blessings of Western culture have not prevented similar atrocities to those nowadays associated with terrorism, some of which were inflicted in the name of the Christian religion and God. The collective memory of migrants may contain references to such experiences, especially in the former colonies. This type of motivation would therefore not serve dialogue with migrant churches.

HEALING

Let us now turn to healing, a regular issue on the dialogue agenda, especially because of the diversity of forms it may take in Pentecostal churches, including migrant churches. Even within the Pentecostal world, healing may be a topic for discussion. Not all churches will practice exorcism, for example. Besides, third-generation churches will have 'domesticated' the 'wilder' forms of healing. The so-called Toronto Blessing caused much debate in Pentecostal circles.

Obviously, if there is one example of a religious phenomenon to which the notion of power as defined above is applicable, it is healing. The healer, using his or her access to sacred resources, changes something in the situation of the person being healed. The latter usually consents with this form of exercising power, although resistance is expressed in the case of exorcism. When a person is healed through sacred power, that power is closely connected with meaning, since the cure occurs in the context of faith, appealing to divine resources that are said to have the power to heal. At the same time, other powers, viewed as forces of evil, are subjected to exorcism and spiritual warfare. In most cases, healing is more than something that happens to the body or the mind. The term also often applies to other aspects of human well-being, including strained personal relationships, poverty, bad luck, difficulties in obtaining a residence permit and other afflictions that people have to deal with. This wider view on healing is consistent with the holistic conviction that faith puts a claim on all aspects and sectors of life, just as evil forces equally threaten these same aspects and sectors.

The field of healing can be viewed as a reflection of the wider struggle for power and meaning that is typical of Pentecostalism, including the type found in migrant churches. The element of migration to another country, in the Western modernized context, thus gives a wider meaning to healing than something that happens to the body or the person. The migrant, having moved out of his or her local home context, becomes acquainted, often in a painful way, with the globalizing world and may therefore be in dire need of a solution to his or her problems. The migrant's situation is the scene of a struggle that has cosmic dimensions. The military metaphors of spiritual warfare and prayer warriors, supported by texts from Scripture, express the connection between the personal and the global. This adds a dimension to the person's affliction, putting him or her into a much wider framework than the closed horizon of the personal affliction appears to suggest. The migrant's individual experience of affliction is connected to the global perspective that he or she is now part of. Despite its Christianized form, this perspective may simultaneously correspond with pre-Christian traditional cosmologies, allowing potential converts to maintain some form of continuity with the past, despite the dramatic rupture of conversion.

A specific meaning that comes with healing practice concerns the role of the community. The worldwide fellowship of believers begins in the local group. Healing often occurs in this social setting, although individual face-to-face situations happen as well. Yet, to the afflicted person, the experience of being adopted by a caring community may be important in overcoming personal trouble, whether corporeal or not. The power of the group as a community is a meaningful part of the person's experience.

Healing is often instrumental in causing conversion. It is a way of preaching and convincing without words. The meaning that the new faith holds for the convert may be derived from the experience of a power that heals. The cosmic dimension of this power may be the extra factor that convinces the convert of taking this personal step. Despite the plurality of the Pentecostal field, including migrant churches, the person may experience that (s)he is part of a bigger whole, a counter-society with the powerful backing of the Spirit. Though converting into a particular church, the conversion also regards the person's worldview, in the literal sense.

Through healing, it also becomes clear that the body occupies a central role in the Pentecostal's experience of his or her faith, despite the stereotypical view that the Pentecostal morals usually promote a strict or even negative view of the body's pleasures, or that the soul is more important than the body, the hereafter of more value than the here and now. Reality does not always obey these stereotypes. Observing one Pentecostal church service is sufficient to discover how Pentecostal believers use their bodies in all stages of their meetings, whether in praise and worship, in prayer, or in singing. The contrast with most mainline services is obvious. Here again – also in migrant churches – converts can be observed in how they draw on their past for traditional forms of using the body. These may be included in the ways that the new faith is expressed and then show some continuity with the past, despite the new life that the convert leads.

Finally, with regard to the dialogue situation, healing may be an issue, especially where mainline churches usually do not see themselves as fit to play a role in this sector of life, at least not in the sense of stimulating a community's practice of using the Spirit's gift of healing. In the context of the asymmetrical relationship that may hamper dialogue, this topic may help to redress the balance. In any case, the question will inevitably be on the agenda.

POWER AND MEANING

In drawing together the different lines elaborated thus far, and looking towards the future of Pentecostal migrant churches, an anthropological consideration of the relationship between power and meaning may be helpful. Despite the selectivity and bias of the discipline, some of the ideas developed in the field of cultural anthropology are in my view enlightening and instructive.

An important distinction that has been mentioned by several of the authors in this book is that between the center and the margin. Correspondingly, power and meaning are differently related, depending on the perspective that is used, either from the center or from the margin. Where power relations are concerned, migrant Pentecostal churches can, as a rule, be classified as belonging much more to the margins than to the center of society, whether national or global. Also within global Christianity, these churches occupy a more marginal than central position. The label 'migrants' expresses movement, being on their way, neither here nor there. The difficulties migrants experience when integrating into the new society also reflects their marginality, in terms of work, housing, health care, residence permits, education, as well as with regard to finding a building or rooms for their church life. In comparison to the mainline churches, migrant churches not only share the outsiders' position with Pentecostal churches, but also with all other migrants. Even after their migration, they are still people on the move. This makes them vulnerable and weak.

A special interest in marginal phenomena has developed in cultural anthropology, especially through the work of Victor Turner (for example, 1969, 1982, 1988). One of the characteristics that define the margin is that, in terms of social structure, the relationships between people are more horizontal than vertical. In other words: power is not an important marker of the margin. People in the margin do not take part in the power center and may, consciously or without perceiving it, remain free of the center's influence. A strong sense of community, or *communitas* as Turner called it, is present in marginal contexts. Temporarily, or sometimes more permanently, the vertical structures are put between brackets. Ritual is one of the places where this communitas may become visible. As Turner shows from his Zambian fieldwork (1969), a society may use ritual and its communitas to overcome conflict and affliction. But marginality – or, as Turner calls it, 'liminality' – may also occur in other sectors of life, accordingly taking specific forms. Religious liminality may therefore be different from economic, social or political liminality, even though there may be links between these diverse forms. Within

these sectors of life, migrants are positioned in a variety of ways, whether volun-
tarily or involuntarily. Their position in one sector may push them to a similar
position in another sector or, by way of compensation, to the exact opposite position. The warm inclusion in a migrant Pentecostal church will counterbalance
and compensate the cold exclusion in other sectors of society. Migrants who are
otherwise excluded, may feel attracted to a migrant church, especially if the
church promises improvement in other sectors of life.

Whereas in the margin the social structure is simple and informal, being even –
as Turner calls it – an anti-structure, the reverse occurs with regard to symbolic
structures. While power relations are reduced to a minimum, the meaning-making is intense and creativity is given maximum opportunity. The fact that social
control is limited, allows for freedom and spontaneity. In religious terms, one
might say that where the kings and priests are temporarily kept silent, the
prophets get all the space they need. In fact, religious movements often find their
start in a power vacuum that allows for new initiatives. The image of the desert
as a place that is marginal to normal society but central to the visionary experience of a religious founder is prominent in more than one world religion (see
Droogers 1980). Interestingly and correspondingly, the first followers occupy
marginal positions in society: poor, women, sick, low caste; in short, in the terms
of Acts 2, the foreigners, the servants and the handmaidens.

Christians will not have difficulty in applying these ideas to the origins of their
religion, just as Pentecostals – and, even more so, the migrants among them –
will recognize marginal traits in the events that surrounded Pentecost. Besides,
weakness and vulnerability are central values to a religion where the divine mes-
senger is, as suggested by one of the authors in this book, a 'wounded healer'
who, for example, offers preferential treatment to the marginalized lepers who
live in the marginal region of Galilee.

Now, where do Pentecostals – and a fortiori the migrants among them – nowadays
stand in this context? In terms of power and meaning, one might say that Pentecostals, at least initially, show several characteristics of the marginal position. The
manifestations of the Spirit are by definition marginal, deviating from the normal
practice. Already in the story from Acts 2, the marginality and abnormality are
evident: 'these men are full of new wine'. I alluded above to the Pentecostal asymmetrical position with regard to mainline churches. Often their position in society
is marginal, especially in Third World countries, with the possible exception of
African churches, which seem to attract many educated lower-middle-class
people. On the other hand, the typical West African phenomenon of the rural
prayer camps reinforces the marginal dimension. Migrants, as already explained,
have extra marginal characteristics that can be added to their status as Pentecostals.

At the same time, it is clear that success and church growth bring with them institutionalization and thereby the need to organize the church's social structure. In Turner's terms, this means that the anti-structure is gradually replaced by a vertical social structure. Correspondingly, the creativity of the marginal position is weakened, simply because the strengthening of the social structure brings more social control and discipline with it. Marketing techniques are being used to run the religious enterprise that is the outcome of the performance of a successful leader. Spontaneity is subjected to routine, codification and effect management. The use of electronic media changes the content and form of the message. 'Human agendas', as one of the authors puts it, may begin to determine church life of what she calls 'mainlined Pentecostalism'. The initial marginal traits are no guarantee for a continued liminality. They are not intrinsic to all churches of the Pentecostal brand and may become absent in established Pentecostal churches. People may even view them as a vehicle for their moving to more central positions in all sectors of life.

The difficult paradox is that the Pentecostal message calls for proclamation but its chances of being heard are lessened as soon as it is widely heard. The dramatic, personal and bodily experience with the power of the Spirit will have difficulty surviving social control. The original Pentecostal faith seems to depend on the marginal condition in which it first arose. Once Pentecostals and their churches and movements leave the margin for the center, the power relations change and, correspondingly, the meaning of the message as well (for an enlightening example, see Johannesen 1995). One may ask whether the global expansion and the use of warfare metaphors do not equally point to such a transfer to the center, just as the promise of wealth does in prosperity-gospel-oriented churches. The entry into politics of some of the larger churches in some countries also appears to point in this direction.

To me, as an anthropologist who is relatively marginal to but nevertheless concerned with Pentecostalism, it seems that the trend in Pentecostalism toward a mainline position will determine its future. The current fame of numerical expansion may make leaders intoxicated with success and blind to the dark side of this shining full moon. Even if solutions are found to the problem of autonomous power mechanisms, of routine, of human agendas, of unfulfilled promises of wealth, of the responsible use of fulfilled promises of wealth, the question remains whether the faithful – and especially the leadership – are really able to remain faithful to the original marginality of Christianity and more particularly of Pentecost. The apparent blessing may prove to be a curse in disguise.

In making this plea, I do not want to romanticize the marginalized status. Nor do I wish to return to a kind of monastic sobriety and exclusiveness. What is much more at stake is the quest for a Christian-Pentecostal way of dealing with power that leaves the meaning of the core message untouched. The quest is for the right identity.

This would necessitate another view on power than the one I have used thus far. Instead of influencing other people's behavior, the core element of this type of power would be the serving position, making oneself 'of no reputation', humble and obedient (Phil 2.7,8). Just as the classical definition of power emphasizes a change that is brought about, the change that this type of power seeks to produce is to serve the promotion of life (see Jacobs 2002, pp. 117-121). The message of Pentecost and the availability of the charismata may very well fit this alternative definition of power. Maybe mainline Christianity, despite its roots in such a view of power, has throughout its history oriented itself too much to the mechanisms represented by the classical definition of power. Successful Pentecostalism risks being mainlined in the same way. Yet, in both cases, hidden in the deeper layers of the Christian heritage, the meanings that may save the flock from this new Fall lie ready to be activated. Many Protestant churches, and Pentecostal churches in particular, have the habit of renewing themselves after a few generations, either by founding a new church after the rediscovery of the original message, or by starting a revival movement within the church, as has happened in the Charismatic renewal. So the experience of a return to the source is there. It may save the Pentecostal churches and movements from asphyxiation by success.

If this view is correct, then the only way to avoid the side effects of the spirit of power is to return to the power of the Spirit. Though this suggestion may be understood theologically, I also mean it in the anthropological sense, in view of Turner's appreciation of the margin with its horizontal and simple social structure, combined with its spontaneity and creativity. If all religion starts with an experience, as is the case of Pentecostalism, then that experience should be saved from institutionalization and domestication. Meaning must control power, not the other way around – with the exception of the Spirit's power. The migrant churches are perhaps privileged in being marginal according to almost all definitions. They may show that it is difficult to domesticate the power of the Spirit, despite the spirit of power.

Acknowledgements
I gratefully acknowledge helpful comments on an earlier version of this article by Birgit Meyer and Regien Smit.

References cited

Droogers, André
1980 'Symbols of Marginality in the Biographies of Religious and Secular Inno-
vators. A comparative study of the lives of Jesus, Waldes, Booth, Kim-
bangu, Buddha, Mohammed and Marx'. In: *Numen* 27(1) pp. 105-121.
2001 'Paradise Lost: The Domestication of Religious Imagination'. In: Don
Handelman and Galina Lindquist, eds., 'Playful Power and Ludic Spaces:
Studies in Games of Life', special issue of *Focaal, European Journal of
Anthropology* 37, pp. 105-119.
2003 'The power dimensions of the Christian community: an anthropological
model'. In: *Religion: a journal of religion and religions* 33/3, pp. 263-280.
2005 'Enjoying an Emerging Alternative World: Ritual in Its Own Ludic Right'.
In: Don Handelman and Galina Lindquist, eds., *Ritual in Its Own Right:
Exploring the Dynamics of Transformation* (New York, Oxford: Berghahn
Books) pp. 138-154. Also published as 'Enjoying an Emerging Alternative
World: Ritual in Its Own Ludic Right'. In: *Social Analysis* 48/2 (2004) pp.
138-154.

Jacobs, E.J.J.
2002 The Feminine Way 'O Jeito Feminino': Religion, Power and Identity in
South Brazilian Base Communities. Amsterdam: PhD Vrije Universiteit.
Johannesen, Stanley
1994 'Third-Generational Pentecostal Language: Continuity and Change in
Collective Perceptions'. In: Karla Poewe (ed.), *Charismatic Christianity as
a Global Culture* (Colombia, South Carolina: University of South Carolina
Press) pp. 175-199.

Turner, Victor W.
1969 *The Ritual Process: Structure and Anti-Structure* (London: Routledge and
Kegan Paul)
1982 *From Ritual to Theatre, The Human Seriousness of Play* (New York: PAJ
Publications)
1988 *The Anthropology of Performance* (New York: PAJ Publications)

Biodata

Anderson, Allan
Co-ordinator of the Research Unit for New Religions and Churches, Centre for Missiology and World Christianity, University of Birmingham, United Kingdom.

Bridges Johns, Cheryl
Professor at the Pentecostal Church of God Theological Seminary, Cleveland, Tennessee (USA).

Droogers, André
Professor in Social and Cultural Anthropology at the Vrije Universiteit (VU) Amsterdam and director of Hollenweger Center.

Himmans Arday, Daniel
Founder-pastor of the African True Teachings of Christ's Temple in Amsterdam Bijlmermeer, experienced in ministry of healing.

Hollenweger, Walter
Reformed theologian and Emeritus Professor of Mission at Birmingham University. Bridge builder between ecumenicals and Pentecostals. In 2003, he offered his library and his research archive to the Hollenweger Center at Amsterdam.

Shaull, Richard (1920 – 2002)
Reformed theologian, educator, author and missionary. Was for many years Professor of Ecumenics at Princeton Theological Seminary, where he articulated a theology of liberation learned from the poor but aimed at liberating mainline Protestants.

Van Beek, Huibert
Former staff member of the World Council of Churches, responsible for relationships with Evangelical, Pentecostal and African Instituted churches and Secretary of the Continuation Committee on the Global Christian Forum.

Van der Kooi, Cornelis
Reformed theologian and associate professor of dogmatics and endowed professor of the Theology of Charismatic Renewal at the Vrije Universiteit (VU) Amsterdam.

Van der Laan, Cornelis
Director of Azusa Theological Seminary and Professor of Pentecostal Studies at the Vrije Universiteit (VU) Amsterdam.

Van der Laan, Paul
Pentecostal theologian and Professor of Religion at Southeastern University, Lakeland, Florida, USA, wrote his doctoral thesis on the ecumenical-Pentecostal dialogue.

Van Laar, Wout
Reformed pastor and Director of the Netherlands Missionary Council (NZR). Worked in the eighties in theological education and pastoral work in Chile.

Währisch-Oblau, Claudia
Pastoral worker and researcher with migrant churches in North-Rhine Westfalia, related to Church of Rhineland and United Evangelical Mission.

Zegwaart, Huibert
Studied theology and philosophy and is Professor of History of Pentecostalism at the Azusa Theological Seminary Amsterdam.

Dépôt légal 4e trimestre 2006 - n° 4328

N° d'impression : 204998